'THERE'S SOMETHING ABOUT WHITECHAPEL'

by Jamie Boyle

www.warcrypress.co.uk

"THERE'S SOMETHING ABOUT WHITECHAPEL... NOT MUCH... BUT SOMETHING"!

Morrissey 2005

ISBN: 978-1-912543-47-2

Printed and bound in Great Britain by the PMM Group, UK.

Book Cover Design by Matthew Oakley

Find out more at facebook.com/warcrypublishing/

DEDICATION

I'd like to dedicate this book to my very own 'Dark Annie', my wife Shirley-Anne Boyle. During the writing of this book, she was battling Kidney cancer and had an operation to remove half her kidney. She is the most tenacious person I've ever met and never shies away from anything life throws at her.

She may only be 5ft nothing but she's a typically tough Yorkshire woman and I'm proud to say she is my bad-ass wife, the Shirbanater!

This book is dedicated to you my darling xx

I'd also like to thank all the staff at James Cook University Hospital who took great care of my wife, especially the staff on Ward 8.

CONTENTS

FOREWORD
BY EDWARD STOW (HISTORIAN)

I grew up in Surrey, so I had never been to the East End until I went to Queen Mary College, part of the University of London, on Mile End Road in the early 1980's. From that temporary situation, I basically just stayed in the area for twenty years. Part of the reason I chose Queen Mary's was because back in the early 1970s my older brother had already read a book about Jack the Ripper, by Daniel Farson. Back then there were only a handful of books available on Jack. It was my brother who was always talking to me about the tiny narrow streets of Whitechapel. When I got to the area myself after talking about it for so long with my brother, I have to say it was exactly as I'd imagined it in my mind.

There are very few places in the world like Whitechapel. It draws you to it and you can feel the events that have taken place there. I've had this strange sort of love affair with the East End ever since. My sons were born at the Royal London Hospital on Whitechapel Road. The traditional East End culture of the place was very appealing when I first arrived. Throughout the 1970s and 80s there was a popular fascination with the East End because of The Sweeney, Minder and all the other chirpy Cockney geezer types, so people wanted to learn more. Over the years I became a sort of surrogate East Ender patriot for the place.

During my student years I would often go back to my parents' place in Surrey, but I'd know when I was back in the East End because inevitably, I would be confronted by some strange and unusual behaviour that could only happen in the East End. For instance, once I stepped off the train when a drunk dosser collapsed in front of me on Commercial Road. As in Jack's era, there are still today an awful lot of doss houses in Aldgate and Whitechapel. On this particular occasion, when I saw this shabby drunk with matted hair and a big red face fall over on the pavement right in front of me like a sack of potatoes, I just thought to myself, 'OK I'm back in the East End now'.

Another odd thing about the East End is there's so many strip bars. Not as many as there used to be but there's a good dozen of them even now. I always marvelled at those tourists that would go to Soho and get ripped off a few hundred quid, yet they could have come to the East End and got the same for a fiver!

Youngsters today in the area talk a bit like "innit" and its gone very much along the 50 Cent New York gangster talk. You don't hear the old Cockney, Minder-like chat with things like, "Oi, you got a score to lend me, son?" That kind of chat finished around 15 or so years ago. You no longer hear the words 'drum' or 'gaff' for a flat, its described as 'yard' as it's all become Americanised in a fake way. Listening to these kids using phrases such as, "ya get me blud innit, wag one bro" - is not a Cockney way at all. I would say the old Cockney way of talking has moved out to Essex.

The area of London I hang around the most is certainly the East End compared to the North, South and West Ends. There's history in the City of London and lots of the West End but nowhere near as much as the East End.

There's just so many layers of real history in the East End. The Labour Party was effectively made in the East End and the whole Labour movement because it's typically working class. The Trade Union movement wouldn't even exist if it wasn't for the East End because it was formed by events in the area very largely, such as the Dock Strikes and the Match Girls Strike. The whole area didn't have any middle-class folk in it, it was all purely the working class who worked on the Docks and markets. The Unions could only have formed when there's a feeling of a community between people who associate with each other.

There's so much interesting architecture in the East End also when you think about it. I do love walking around the remains of what's left and the traces of the Docks, for it to really sink in about what it was like in the place once upon a time. It's similar to reading an old manuscript when I see the old buildings, roads and houses of yesteryear. When you look at the old Whitechapel Bell Foundry then you go further up the road to see something very modern, the change over time really dawns on you. It always astounds me to think that the Liberty Bell in Philadelphia was made in Whitechapel Bell Foundry, then around the corner is the great big mosque in Whitechapel, and at the back of that, built into the walls, there's the remains of a synagogue. Whitechapel, and the East End as a whole is one interesting place, I know because I lived there for a long time.

If you'd like to get in touch with Edward, you can via -

YOUTUBE – The House of Lechmere
FACEBOOK – The House of Lechmere

INTRODUCTION
Jamie Boyle - Author

I'd like to start off this book by saying by no means am I any kind of Jack the Ripper/East End expert. That kind of title goes to the likes of Richard Jones (the No.1 on this planet in my opinion), Donald Rumbelow, Robin Odell, Frogg Moody, Stewart P Evans, Paul Begg, Martin Fido (God rest him), Mick P Priestley, Phil Hutchinson, Adam Wood, Edward Stow and Lindsay Siviter. Those people are the ones who've dedicated a good chunk of their lives looking into the Whitechapel murders of 1888 and I take my hat off to each and every one of them. Those guys have brought me so much material over the years to study and I thank them for that.

Me, myself I'm more of a curious writer focusing on a subject way out of my depth, but with a lot of energy, passion and focus on this story. The names above I have admired from a far for such a long time.

Although, I am a professional writer for a living, this book was one I wrote for myself because I have a personal genuine interest. I've always been engrossed with the Whitechapel story from 1888 for as long as I can remember. I first became aware of the Whitechapel fiend purely by accident. I was around 10 or 11 and came across the film 'Jack the Ripper' on the telly, which had been released 3 years prior in 1988 to mark the centenary of those horrendous crimes. To be honest I was being sent to bed by my parents and as I was leaving the front room, I saw the film starting so I started asking my mother who was this Jack the murderer etc... When I watched that fantastic movie starring Michael Caine, back then it's so easy to think at the end, 'oh we know who the killer was now it was old Sir William Gull with his dodgy coach driver John Netley all along, search over and crime solved'! Well, I'm sorry to say that it may have been solved in the film but in reality, it wasn't, but that's what makes this whole story so bloody enthralling.

As I got older and looked into it more the whole theory of the film was of course ridiculous, but it sold books 100 years after the murders ended. The theory of the film was never seriously considered even back in that autumn of terror in 1888. It's totally ludicrous when you look at the whole case that the Queen's doctor, who in fact had had a stroke around this period, was dragging prostitutes into his carriage and butchering them all over the East End but it did make a bloody brilliant film however.

After first coming across that film, it left me with an insane thirst to find out more about who really was the evil knife-wielding maniac with a catchy nickname but whose name nobody in the world knew even 103 years on from that point. Looking back, I must have been such a strange child to have been in the last year of primary school and going in library's sitting there looking at books of Jack the Ripper. The reality of it was the children's aisle with Bart Simpson and Teenage Mutant Ninja Turtles didn't appeal to me as I hovered around the North Ormesby adult sections I wasn't really even supposed to be in. In my last year of Primary school in St Alphonsus we had a fancy-dress party at Christmas. Most kids went as The Karate Kid, Wee Willie Winky or a footballer, I went as Freddy Krueger!

After I had read everything, I could on Jack the Ripper, I then started reading about The Yorkshire Ripper Peter Sutcliffe, then in 1993 I watched The Krays movie starring Martin & Gary Kemp the pop stars from Spandau Ballet and overnight I was hooked. My next aim was to go to Berwick Hills library and dig out all the books I could on my new found obsession Ronnie & Reggie Kray whilst nicking off school from St Anthony's.

Back in 1993 there were very few books on The Krays, I think they became more well known when the internet took off and from that there came more books and more films. This coincided with the death in 1995 of Ronnie Kray and for the next five years the cry was, 'FREE REGGIE KRAY' from much of the media.

One of the only books which was out in the early days was 'The Profession of Violence' by John Pearson (who has sadly passed away recently) which in my opinion is the very best book out of around seventy plus that are available these days. The reason that one is the most accurate is that it was released in 1972, only a few years on from their reign of terror being brought to an end by Judge Melford Stevenson in the famous Court No.1 at The Old Bailey. Judge Stevenson told the brothers that society had earned a rest from their activities, and he threw the key away on the wideboy East Enders. He passed a sentence of life with a recommendation of thirty years which meant that the Kray brothers lives as free men came to an end at the tender age of 34 at least until they were old age pensioners.

The other books available to me were 'Our Story' by Fred Dinenage and 'My Story' by Ron Kray. As I sat in Berwick Hills library staring at the black & white photos of the twins most days as I was wagging school, I knew I had a fascination with the true crime genre. Some may have called it unhealthy, but I was interested in what made these people tick, it was so far removed from anything I'd seen growing up. I'm still as interested today at 42 years old as I was 30 odd years ago. I feel when you have an interest in true crime or write about it for a living as I do, I often find myself explaining why I'm fascinated with some of the dark characters that I am. I just like to try and understand about human nature. I don't think there's anything clever or glamourous about the Kray twins walking into pubs and shooting people stone dead. I don't think there's anything to romanticise about a crazed lunatic running around the streets of Whitechapel and butchering them poor innocent women who have forever been embedded in East End folklore forevermore for such a reason. Those poor unfortunates' names would have long been forgotten had they not met their fate at the end of Jack's knife and for that it's granted them immortal life in the history books of true crime.

I try to understand what would actually makes a person behave like that, what could have possibly gone so wrong in one's life to indulge in such evil, because he was having a bad day? Or was it just a macabre hobby? Were they abused, bullied or suffered so much that the only way to make themselves feel better was to go out and take the life of some poor innocent soul?

Today in 2022 there's 283 Waterstones scattered all over Great Britain. Their most popular genre I can assure you is True Crime, so what does that tell you about human nature?! Is it any different to the ghouls who paid one penny to go into the homes of residents on Hanbury street to gawk at the bloody murder scene where Jack the Ripper's second victim Annie Chapman was ripped apart on September 9th, 1888? In my opinion I don't think it is!

Of course, the Whitechapel killings were 134 years ago and it's that distance of time that has given in to some acceptability of 'tourism' for want of a better term, and that's because it was about five generations ago. For example, you wouldn't go to Leeds/Bradford today and see a 'Yorkshire Ripper tour' and very rightly so. Today it's known as 'dark tourism' and the harsh reality is murder sells and there's been a whole industry built up to try and identify Jack.

Since I came across Jack the Ripper and the Kray twins at such an early age, I've always had a massive love for London, particularly the East End. Over the years I've had so many visits to London and have had no interest in visiting the North, South and West parts, I've only wanted to be in the East for it has so much iconic history.

Away from Jack the Ripper and the Krays, the East End has so many other traits that interests me in life such as pugilism. The East End was the concrete jungle which many top fighters such as Lenny McLean, Roy Shaw, Billy Walker, John H Stracey, Charlie Magri, Jimmy Flint, John L Gardner, Nigel Benn, Mark Kaylor and Kevin Mitchell have all fought their way out of. In the East End people never had anything so their only way to rise from the slums was to fight their way to the top. Ray Winstone the top film star is another boy from the East End who's done good and he's one of a very few who's done well from the area.

Away from the sport of boxing, which we'll come back to further on in the book, the place was a hotspot for the famous playwriter Oscar Wilde. Although Wilde lived in Chelsea, West London he was often seen in the East End where he would often pick up a male companion for the night. At the end of the 19th century homosexuality was illegal and looked upon as the same as paedophilia. Of course, Wilde was imprisoned for his sex life and sentenced to two years hard labour in Pentonville. It's even been speculated that there was a connection between Oscar Wilde and Jack the Ripper and Wilde even sheds light on his identity in his play "The Picture of Dorian Gray".

In that same Oscar Wilde/Jack the Ripper period you had Joseph Merrick aka The Elephant Man, walking up Whitechapel High Street daily with a bag over his head. In this same period Bram Stoker who created Dracula and Lewis Carroll who wrote Alice in Wonderland will have been around the East End also. Carroll has even been suggested as being a Ripper suspect himself and maybe one of the most absurd suggestions to help sell books over the last hundred plus years.

Often when my friends go on holiday abroad to sunny locations, I can never understand it. I can fully understand that famous Samuel Johnson quote which is in this book more than anyone.

Today in the 21st century if Jack the Ripper or even the Kray twins for that matter came and looked around their old manor's they would find them completely unrecognisable. Today there's every religion, race and culture if you walk along the vibrant Whitechapel High Street. A little further on you have Brick Lane and if you walk up that road feeling a little peckish then you'll have to walk past over sixty curry houses, and as you walk past each one a member of staff will come out and use his best salesman patter to lure you in, very much like the 'lucky lucky men' abroad who try to sell you their bits of tack.

One of those curry houses on Brick Lane was once 'The Frying Pan', it is the building where Jack the Ripper's first victim Mary Ann Nichols spent the night drinking. If you look to the top of that building, you can see 'The Frying Pan' in the old brickwork.

I was lucky enough to spend some time with, in my opinion the world's No.1 Jack the Ripper expert in the summer of 2021. That week I was in London I was down to meet a few famous people such as Shaun Attwood, MMA fighter Alex Reid and former Celtic manager Martin O'Neill but I was more starstruck meeting Mr

Jones than any other person because of my interest in the Whitechapel killings. Richard even told me that the town of Middlesbrough had its own link to the Whitechapel murders which did surprise me. Richard told me more and although this may sound very strange, I was kind of flattered that the place I grew up in had its own link to the greatest criminal mystery the world has ever known. I'll explain the Middlesbrough/Jack the Ripper link further on in the book.

The venerable Richard and I walked all over the East End, and he told me that although the East End has changed such a lot, if you look around closely, there's many of the original bits of the East End there exactly like that 'Frying Pan' pub sign in the bricks. Little clues to its history are everywhere.

The Kray twins ruled the roost in the East End before they were taken off the streets by the authorities in May 1968. If they were still around today, I don't think there would be many that would listen to them, half of the people in the East End don't speak English so they wouldn't take any notice to the two tasty geezers who owned the local snooker hall, the East End has become so busy and much bigger over the years.

When I walk around the streets of Bow, Whitechapel, Shoreditch, Spitalfields, Bethnal Green, Mile End & Wapping and I look up to the historic buildings I'm just totally in awe of the history behind them. Once upon a time I know that the scene was one of little boys with mucky faces on each street corner screaming in their proper cockney accents, "MURDER MURDER IN WHITECHAPEL... RIPPER STRIKES AGAIN... TERROR IN LONDON" as they're selling copies of The Star in their flat 8-piece caps and raggy clothes. In fact, the first ever paper to sell a million copies in one day did so with the crimes of Jack the Ripper on the front page. Joseph Merrick would be walking up and down Whitechapel High Street with a limp and just part of the Whitechapel furniture. In actual fact for two years Merrick was earning a living at No. 259 (now a saree shop) as part of a freak show. Long before Match of the Day came about people would pay to enter these places and stare at these poor unfortune souls who all had deformities of some sort. Sadly, for those people deemed as freaks it was the only way to make a living and it was before modern day medicine could do what it does today in the 21st century.

Regarding the sex trade, it wasn't like today where these girls sell themselves for usually only two reasons, one being heroin and the other being crack cocaine, these girls had to sell themselves just to have a bed for the night in one of the many doss houses across the East End, or to put some stale bread on the table for their family to eat.

The doss houses were filthy! The conditions would usually be full of the previous occupier's urine, faeces, blood, body lice or vomit among the wooden beds filled with straw. No wonder that everybody was kaylied on gin because their lives were so deeply depressing. I'm not talking about the gin which we drink today, I'm talking about gin which would be made in bathtubs and take the lining off your stomach no problem. This drink which was so potent could make a man go blind and the Whitechapel residents used to drink it in the pints. Think about the crystal meth epidemic in America a decade or so ago then gin and Whitechapel folk were the same. It's no coincidence that this type of gin made your teeth drop out and several of Jack the Rippers victims had hardly a tooth in their head. The ladies of the night would also be hovering around the streets selling flowers to earn that etc bit of income before going back out to sell themselves on those cold, dark and damp streets of London's

East End. Times were that dire often in 1888 that old grandma had to go out and sell herself and nobody thought anything less of her for it.

There are many things that enthral me about Whitechapel, and it will always be one of my favourite places on earth. As I walk around those streets, which was the centre of the Jewish community back in the 19th century, for me it's filled with yesteryears history and I'm like a kid in a sweetshop taking everything in. If I walk around the Northeast, I usually have headphones on, but when I'm in the East End I don't, I'm far too busy noticing everything because I'm so literally obsessed with the whole manor even though today it's often tarred with a bad tag with crime, drugs and antisocial behaviour on the rise.

As a man who's grown up in the North of England, I find the cockney's absolutely gripping to study. I'm like David Attenborough when he studies the gorillas from a distance. Life in London is so much faster than up North. Life almost seems speeded up to the point that nobody has any time for each other, even though everyone knows each other among the many hectic businesses scattered around the very plush East End today.

Back in the day of Jack the Ripper, London was known as the richest city on earth, however in Whitechapel you couldn't get any lower in civilisation, that's how Whitechapel was regarded. The place at that time, was a breeding ground for crime and other poor behavioural habits including muggings, prostitution and brutal assaults. I dare say in that generation if you didn't have your wits about you like the Artful Dodger from Oliver Twist, then you would have been a victim every single day of your life. The streets of the East End were unimaginably dirty and fresh food was hard to come by. The whole place was hard to live in with the awful smell of pollution and sewage in the air. At one point the smell was that bad in the East End it was brought up in the Houses of Commons and discussed among the government politicians, they said that it was that bad during low tide that they thought about moving parliament to somewhere fresher shall we say.

These days you can walk up Fournier Street in Spitalfields and you can see houses that would sell for several millions of pounds, the complete opposite to how it was in Jack the Ripper's era when as many as 15 would be living in the one room! These days areas such as Spitalfields is a pretty trendy place to live in London and if the residents of the Jack the Ripper era where here today they'd never believe it. Who would have thought that if you put a time machine and moved on over a hundred-plus years that many of the top films have been shot there, films that have featured the likes of Angelina Jolie and top British series' such as Downtown Abbey and Luther?

To be quite honest writing this book was a snap decision I made in October 2021 at 5am in the morning. I actually woke my wife up to tell her I was going to write about Whitechapel and all that captivated me about it. To say she wasn't amused is an understatement, but I felt it just had to be done. I felt so strongly about it so here goes.

Whitechapel will always be my little place where I can escape the pressures from the Northeast at least once a year for the rest of my days. This is my silly little quirky book on Whitechapel because I just simply bloody had to. The story of the Whitechapel murders from 1888 – 1891 are the ultimate who done it, but there will never quite be an ending, I truly believe we will never know who the villain was.

"When a man is tired of London, he is tired of life; for there is in London all that life can afford."

Samuel Johnson

CHAPTER 1
THE WHITECHAPEL KILLINGS

If Jack the Ripper was essentially a media creation, the bodies left behind were very real. His name is a metaphor for terror, violence and brutality. His onslaught against the downtrodden of London has rarely been equalled for savagery. We only know of him as Jack the Ripper, and some say that he came from Hell.

In 1888 the manor of Whitechapel was home to the wretched and where disease and degradation prevailed. It was a place where horror and more lurked around every corner! In the late 19th century, the area of Whitechapel had around 900,000 people living in it alone, up to 50,000 of that number were Jewish. It's a far cry from today with the much smaller number of 15,000 living in the area. That gives you an idea of just how overcrowded it was.

The vicious circles of bad behaviour the district offered among the dirty streets for the unfortunates who had to live there don't bare thinking about. Everything they owned was carried in their pockets, there were no safe places to put anything.

The series of Whitechapel murders are the Everest of British true crime. These monstrous events happened in the East End which is the dark heart of London. The killings are the greatest mystery in the entire history of British crime because no one was ever caught! Everybody loves a 'who done it' and the Jack the Ripper spree is the original one because there are simply so many suspects.

Today in 2022, and over 134 years on, there's as many as over 200 suspects and in my opinion as many as 15-20 serious candidates. I could present a case for each of those top culprits, where after looking over evidence, albeit circumstantial because of the lack of DNA evidence back then, I could think, well that's it, solved! Then I could sit and think about the next suspect, and it would blow my original theory out of the water and again it would be a case of by jove you've got it old chap!

All murders of the canonical five victims Mary Ann Nichols, Annie Chapman, Elizabeth Stride, Catherine Eddowes and Mary Jane Kelly all happened in the space of exactly ten weeks. The reality is that there were more than five victims as there was eleven unsolved murders in total but because they weren't deemed to have been murdered by the same hands as the canonical five the other six often don't get a mention.

Sir Arthur Conan Doyle created the fictional detective Sherlock Holmes the year before the Whitechapel Murders and although it set a scene the Sherlock stories were just that, fictional. The horrors that went on in Whitechapel were very real. The first slaying happened in April 1888 and the last was in the February of 1891. It's tragic that history overlooks Francis Coles, Annie Farmer, Ada Wilson, Martha Tabram, Alice McKenzie, Emma Smith and the Pinchin Street torso that was tragically never identified. In total there was 11 unsolved murders in 34 months and because nobody was ever brought to justice for any of them no one can safely say that their lives weren't extinguished by one killer or by several.

The district of Whitechapel was the perfect hunting ground for Jack with very few gas lamps on the manor and so many dark alleys into which he could swiftly disappear. All the victims were ladies who were considered to be some of the dregs of society but in truth they had just fallen on hard times. These are the poor lost souls of Whitechapel who've never found peace in death because nobody was held accountable for their savage murders. In my opinion most people think the Jack the Ripper case is just about the five main murders and when you've read about them then that's it. I personally can reassure you that it's much more than that. It's about a whole era, the way the Victorian folk lived, went about their business and still managed to have a smile on their faces in the bleakest of times. As I told you in my introduction, I've been virtually obsessed with true crime my whole life, but nothing has gripped me quite as much as the Whitechapel murders.

Regardless of who really was responsible for these ghastly murders, the history books tell us all that it was a tall man with a snow-white complexion, shark-like dark eyes, dressed in black, wearing a top hat, carrying a cane, pocket watch dangling from a waistcoat and a Gladstone bag full of extremely sharp medical instruments. If you've watched films about him then wherever he walked around the East End in the black of night almost cat-like, a cloud of fog surrounded his whole body! There MUST be that foggy effect when you're portraying Jack because it's in the small print. In fact, if someone fitting that description had walked up to a prostitute at St Botolph's church, Aldgate (aka Prostitute Church) and approached them then that girl would have screamed the East End down and all the attention would have gone to the potential murderer. The reality of it was that whoever Jack the Ripper was, then he'd have probably had the appearance of an international sailor as many confirmed this. His appearance to several witnesses was that he was a man of 5ft 6 to 5ft 7 in height, stocky build, dark moustache and a peak cap with red neckerchief. Maybe this will come as a shock, and it almost spoils the myth but it's a far cry to how the films and documentaries describe him.

Going back to St Botolph's Church, which stands at the junction of Houndsditch and Aldgate High Street. The church has been there since the 7th century and as many as 200 working girls would circle the holy building back in 1888 looking for business. Back in those days there was a rule, as long as the sex-worker never approached the customer and kept moving then she wasn't breaking any laws. As soon as Jack the Ripper killed Liz Stride on Berner Street (now Henriques Street) on the night of the double event and he failed in his first attempt to mutilate the poor woman as he was thought to have been disturbed, he knew that 0.7 of a mile and a 15-minute walk away he was going to find a victim at 'prostitute church' and he did so, only 45 minutes later with Catherine Eddowes. The really sad thing for me was fate played a cruel hand with Catherine Eddowes on the night of her death as the police had earlier released her from custody. Catherine had been arrested for drunken behaviour at 8.30pm on Aldgate High Street for pretending to be a fire engine whilst running up and down the street. What a sense of humour she most has had! After a few hours in police custody Catherine was released close to 1am, with less than one hour to live and nowhere to go her only option was to go back out on the hard streets. Before she left her arresting officer her last words to PC George Hutt were, "goodnight old cock" and off she went to St Botolph's Church where she would meet Jack the Ripper. Ironically Catherine had even joked to friends in the previous weeks that she wasn't frightened of the Whitechapel killer and that he'd better pray that he didn't bump into her.

When you take into account all of those poor woman's plights then each you listen to is sadder than the last. Mary Ann Nichols, Annie Chapman, Liz Stride, Catherine Eddowes and Mary Jane Kelly weren't out putting themselves in grave danger for drug money or personal greed like some sex-workers today in the

London area. Every time I visit London, I often see fliers scattered around for all of these hot, young babes who want to spend the night with you etc... Those lost souls of Whitechapel were doing it for the 4 pence it would cost in the nearest 'doss house' or a glass of gin to numb their senses. Unfortunately for them there was no benefit system like there is today who is going to at least try to put them up in a B & B if there is no other suitable accommodation. The harsh reality was nobody was interested in their sad stories. No one was coming to feel sorry for them or to rescue them. Can you imagine a fate as bleak as if you don't sleep with some fat smelly stinking butcher then you'll have to sleep somewhere as dark, cold and lonely as Itchy Park which was the churchyard for Christ Church in Spitalfields?

Incidentally, another tie for Whitechapel is when Tottenham Hotspur legend Jimmy Greaves, who was the greatest goal scorer England has ever seen, retired from playing in the 1970's he was allegedly often seen boozing in Itchy Park all day with the alcoholics.

The park would also later inspire the Cockney rockers, The Small Faces to write a song in the summer of 1967 which was of course their smash hit, 'Itchy coo Park'.

Some say that the first of the five to be murdered, Mary Ann Nichols, had only been working as a prostitute for a mere two months. I've always found that a hard one to take considering her lasting legacy for all eternity is Mary Ann Nichols the prostitute. Jack's second known victim poor Annie Chapman was literally already dying when she was murdered in a backyard on Hanbury Street in the early hours of September 8th 1888. Doctors confirmed at her autopsy that she wouldn't have seen the year out as she was suffering long standing lung disease, yet she still dragged herself to Commercial Road where it's thought she met

Jack the Ripper, before she brought him to a quiet place where they wouldn't be interrupted. Another sad factor to these ladies' deaths was essentially all five showed Jack where the safest place to murder them would be! The girls basically showed Jack the safest place in the East End to murder them so he wouldn't be interrupted. Liz Stride is often referred to by Ripperologists as 'lucky Liz' because she only had her throat cut compared to all the other girls who were cut up atrociously. One would hardly call it lucky, but you get the point! Another name Elizabeth Stride gets is, 'long Liz' which is also hard to understand as Stride was only 5ft tall. Many ripper experts have said that Liz Stride wasn't in actual fact a ripper victim but a domestic abuse victim. I think it's clear to see that Stride was a victim of The Rippers when you look at all the evidence the history books give you. Neither can I imagine there were many deranged psychopaths going around within such a small space of London, within less than an hour and with the same m.o. of having her throat cut. Catherine Eddowes was found in Mitre Square and the finding officer said that she looked like an open pig in a market. The last of the canonical five was a beautiful young Irish girl called, Mary Jane Kelly aged 25. She's the one we know the least about out of all Jack's victims. The very same week that Jack slaughtered Mary Jane Kelly, Glasgow Celtic Football Club had been founded to feed the poor Irish immigrants in the East End of Glasgow. Beautiful Mary, unlike the other four, was a lot younger and the drink hadn't ravaged her as much as it had the other girls. Mary Jane was brutally butchered in her little room at 13 Millers Court which was just off Dorset Street. If Jack was saving his most heinous act till last on purpose, then he really made a statement by looking at the murder scene, which Inspector Frederick Abberline's men were greeted with that autumn morning. If the house of horrors wasn't bad enough one of the first officers on the scene slipped over on the blood, another was brought to tears and vomited at such a bloody sight the likes of which could only have been cause by sheer evilness.

Mary's body was found at 10.45am by Thomas Bowyer who had been sent by Mary's landlord as she was six weeks behind with her rent, he found her and told the police it looked like the work of the devil as he peered through Mary's broken side window. What he saw is widely acknowledged as the first ever scene of the crime photos.

The whole of London was in a state of shock at the sheer savagery but nobody at the time knew as bad as it was, that day, Jack had committed his most evil act and his reign of terror had come to an abrupt end. Jack didn't only claim the victims we know about, one lady from Hanbury Street was so depressed over all the murders that she committed suicide. However officially the Whitechapel area in total had eleven unsolved murders on it's the file was closed and put away in 1892, four years after the murders started. With no more leads and the murders finally coming to an end the files were put away on a dusty self at Scotland Yard, no doubt the intention being for somebody to finally come back to solve this great mystery at some point.

As the years went by ridiculous myths were tied to the murders. Outrageous suspects snowballed as the years turned into decades and everyone had a theory on who really was the Whitechapel fiend. Many of them completely ludicrous such as Sherlock Holmes author Sir Arthur Conan Doyle, Royal's such as Prince Albert Victor, Jill the Ripper (a female killer), artist Walter Sickert or James Maybrick and his diary. I've even read that playwright Oscar Wilde was the ripper! As I said in the introduction, you could quite easily look at the evidence and be convinced that as many as 20 Jack the Rippers all fit the bill and that's why this case separates itself from any other murder mystery in time. To quote the world's No.1 Jack the Ripper expert Richard Jones, "in regard to Jack the Ripper killings the only thing you can be sure of is we can't be sure of anything."

Everyone is a suspect! I know that Queen Victoria strongly believed that Jack was either a butcher or cattle drover. Queen Victoria followed the case closely and even offered a pardon to any accomplice to the murders if he told all but it was to no avail.

One fact though is that all the murders took place at weekends or early in the morning, which suggests he had a normal job during the week. After the killings he left the scene leaving no evidence. There were no eyewitnesses to his slayings, only dead bodies. The harsh reality of it is now all of this is 134 years on, and Jack the Ripper's identity is something we'll NEVER truly know 100% for sure. Over the years the experts have said that serial killers always kill their first victim in the location they feel the most comfortable in and that he could have lived around Bucks Row (now Durward Street). If he didn't live around there, then he definitely was familiar to the area in my opinion. In fact, all of Jack's victims lived and died within one square mile.

Whoever it was though came from the pits of burning hell and showed the 19th century a pure evil it had never seen before. Although many think Jack was a deranged madman who got lucky, my theory was he was more of a mastermind than a madman. This was the work of a deranged genius as I find it impossible to think he was that lucky at least five times then would vanish into the London fog. Whoever this evil monster was he came out in the dark, murdered in the dark and vanished in the dark. If ever there was an environment for Jack to go about his business, then Whitechapel was perfect i.e., so many dark alleys and passages to vanish into. I've watched and studied the case long enough now to be of the opinion that whoever he was he never did all of that and got away with it on good luck alone. Even if it was solved tomorrow with sufficient evidence, I don't think it would be believed and I think many wouldn't want it solving because it would be spoiling the greatest 'who done it' the world has ever known! There would be no more long debates about it that's for sure. Also, what was the reason that the killer stopped? In my opinion he must have died, got locked up or moved away because killers of this nature don't just think, well I'm pretty bored of this now, I think I'll retire! The fact of the matter is that the police were never close to charging anyone at any stage of their enquiries. For those ten weeks in 1888, the residents of Whitechapel became like TV reality stars of their era, the eyes of the world were on them. Jack was a serial killer 90 years before the term was even used! Science simply wasn't ready for what he brought.

"No one has the ability to laugh at their misfortunes like the women of the East End."

Philip Ridley

CHAPTER 2
A BUSINESS WHICH MAKES A KILLING

Today in 2022 if you go take a look around Whitechapel, Aldgate or Spitalfields on an evening on any given night of the week you'll see several Jack the Ripper tours. Many different groups with people from all over the world all eager and keen to listen to their group leader, who is usually a Ripperologist with a vast knowledge of the occurrences of 1888. The term Ripperologist first came about in the 1980s and it was first used by the old TV personality Jeremy Beadle in a documentary, it has stuck and is used when talking about people who have studied Jack and who earn their living writing or talking about him, sometimes both. Often many tour leaders dress in Victorian dress to add that extra effect on their tour, often carrying a folder to show you snaps of gruesome murder scenes as the area has changed so much now, along with some of the street names. This business, let me tell you is still in very high demand today almost 134 years on from the murders. I know from being on many tours myself, and speaking to several Jack the Ripper guides, that it's not only Joe Public that is interested in the Whitechapel murders, but also some of the biggest celebrities, footballers and actors you could mention.

Although none of us know what he looked like, people will often dress up as Jack the Ripper at Halloween. Today if you look all over the East End, you'll find things such as a fish & chip shop called, 'Jack the Chipper' on Whitechapel High Street. Many of the residents around and also in Greenwich where there's another chippy of the same name was up in roar, all complaining to their local council's that these premises were glamourising serial killers. Something very similar is the 'Jack the Clipper'

Turkish barbers' franchise (their motto is born to bleed) around Bow Lane, Brick Lane, Mayfair, Spitalfields and Canary Wharf parts of the city. Among Jack the Ripper walks, chip shops and barbers there's also the Jack the Ripper Museum on Cable Street in Aldgate. Jack the Ripper has also made it to the London Dungeons and Madame Tussauds waxworks. Although there's no waxwork of him because we don't know what he looked like, there is however a creepy shadow which portrays Jack. Then there's all the Jack the Ripper films which started in 1927 with Alfred Hitchcock's 'The Lodger'. In 1953 a filmed called 'Man in the Attic' where a landlady suspects she has rented a room to the Whitechapel killer. 1959 then saw the release of the film which was simply called 'Jack the Ripper. 1979 saw 'Murder by Decree' come out where Sherlock Holmes investigates the murders committed by Jack but discovers there's a conspiracy to protect the killer. Most people are aware of the films 'Whitechapel' with Michael Caine in it and 'From Hell' with Johnny Depp but there are so many other films out there based around Jack I haven't mentioned. Then there's the BBC drama Whitechapel and countless documentaries. Youngsters are now playing computer games such as Assassin's Creed and Jack the Ripper features on that also. On one hand you can relate to the Whitechapel community who campaign against the chip shops opening and The Ten Bells, Spitalfields and White Hart pubs having the Jack the Ripper theme, or you can think that it's part of the area's social history whether people like it or not. As I told you further back in the book, the first newspaper ever to reach a million sales in one day did so with the Jack the Ripper headlines on the front page. It may have sent the whole of Victorian London in sheer panic but down on Fleet Street, well, bloody murder was good for business.

Back in 1888 the whole world's attention was fully on that little place in the Eastend of London called Whitechapel and that's a fact! Not only are the Whitechapel killings the greatest who done it ever in British crime but it's also very much a true story and nobody can dispute that, however high emotions run about it. Whether people like it or not, Jack the Ripper and his list of victims is big business. It doesn't matter that he was voted the worst Brit ever in British history, beating fascist Oswald Mosley to the title in 2006, because whilst there is still a great interest, there will always be people like myself producing bits and pieces about it and I don't think that's going to stop in our lifetime. For sure in 2088, when we're 200 years on and me, you and all the others are all dead and gone the interest in who really was the monster of London will still be as it is today in 2022. Although today there's no psychopath going around butchering women, Whitechapel is still a far cry from say, Richmond which is widely regarded as the safest part of the city and has the lowest crime count. Regardless of its era, the whole of the Eastend will always be linked to Jack the Ripper and other baddies, people such as the Jack 'spot' Comer, Jack Sheppard aka "Honest Jack" who was a notorious thief in the 1700's, Spring-heeled Jack (mythical demon from 1800's) and the Kray Twins. The masses will always travel from as far as China to come to sample the East End. Jack has simply been made a part of English life. A folk tale of human cruelty which stems from the brutal society of its time. Not only has there been hundreds of books (some by folk as far as Australia and Japan), films and documentaries but there's the songs about Jack from world renowned pop stars such as Screaming Lord Sutch, Motorhead, Morrissey, The White Stripes, My Chemical Romance, LL Cool J, The Sharks, The Duellers and Nick Cave & The Bad Seeds. There was actually even a rock group in France called 'Jack the Ripper'.

Then there's even been Jack the Ripper – The Musicals. All of this would have sounded the sickest thing ever in the world back in 1888 but of course everyone from that time is now dead and it's fallen into folklore mythologically which deems it acceptable to most.

Over the last twenty years or so since the internet has taken off, I've seen people having Jack the Ripper tattoos. People now make their living from telling the Jack the Ripper story and even Ripperologist Richard Jones often says in his interviews to the media, "well Jack the Ripper bought my house." If you log onto any of the biggest platforms in the world such as eBay and Amazon and type in, 'Jack the Ripper' then you'll find everything from Jack the Ripper mugs, keyrings, pin badges, fridge magnets, posters, mugs, picture frames, shirts, toy figures with a hat and cape on, engraved coins, fragrance oils, pretend toy kidneys in a box, fancy dress costumes, stickers etc... The world simply can't get enough of Jack and the Jack PR train seems to still be going and going from strength to strength.

Jack the Ripper to Whitechapel is what Billy the Kid was to the Wild West, Dracula is to Transylvania, Robin Hood to Nottingham and the Loch Ness Monster is to Scotland. Although nobody in the world truly knows what Jack looked, he's part of the territory when it comes to the Whitechapel manor.

The only positive note to come from these horrendous senseless murders was Jack forced the government to make the district of Whitechapel better! If there was any good to come from these monstrosities, then it was only this.

"One day men will look back and say gave birth to the twentieth century."

Jack the Ripper

CHAPTER 3
THE REAL EAST END AND THE CHIRPY COCKNEY

When I think of the old proper Cockney I think of Alf Garnett in his claret & blue scarf screaming, "COME ON WEST HAM." The Hammers are the chosen team of the East Enders because the other options of the manor, Leyton Orient and Dagenham & Redbridge aren't so appealing. I think of the typical London cabbie who never uses a full stop in his vocabulary. I think of EastEnders actress Anita Dobson who played Angie Watts in Eastenders, she is a proper East Ender as she hails from Stepney and her voice is as Cockney as they come. I imagine all of Jack's victims would have spoken exactly like her. I think of the chirpy Cockney bloke who shouts, "AWIGHT" like Michael Barrymore did in his prime, when he signs his autograph, he always signs it with, 'BE LUCKY' like Stepney hardman Roy Shaw also used to do. The stereo type Cock-er-ney geezer wears a baker boy hat and walks very fast usually with a paper under his arm. Sometimes he jumps and clicks his heels together whilst mid-air. He is a proud Londoner as he struts his stuff along the manor. The old London knees-up's like 'Maybe It's Because I'm A Londoner' or 'Doing the Lambeth Walk' are his ring entrances to life in general. I also think of jellied eels, pie & mash, Chas & Dave, smelly boxing gyms, Danny Dyer, Cockney rhyming slang, The Bow Bells, The York Hall (the home of British boxing) and Micky Flanagan doing his proper Cock-er-ney walk on stage whilst strutting around purposely like an arsehole. I think of Lee Mack the other comedian doing his London gag where he says some people are sooo Cock-er-ney it looks like it hurts and that being Northern must be so much easier! In actual fact the true Cockney is a dying breed. Many of the real Eastenders I'm told, moved out to Kent or Essex in the 1970's and left the area.

When I'm in London and I really want to sample the East End, I just go and sit in Pellicci's on Bethnal Green Road and observe. That little wonderland place in the East End has been run by the same lovely Italian family since 1900. The wooden décor you see in it has been there since 1946 but it still looks like it was done last week. Over the years I've met many celebrities in there from football agent Eric Hall, Kray members Chris Lambrianou, boxer Jimmy Flint (the Wapping Assassin), EastEnders actor Nabil Elouahabi and Princess Di actress Elizabeth Debicki. Pellicci's is world famous and so many stars pop along to sample the proper East End, not the drama on the BBC. Up on the walls of Pellicci's there are many pictures of so many world-famous stars. The hospitality in Pellicci's is second to none, I would recommend it to anyone if you wanted to sample a little bit of the old East End.

The old saying goes that you're not a proper Cockney unless you're born within earshot of the sound of The Bow Bells. Often people think the Bow Bells must be in the area Bow near Mile End but it's actually not. The Bow Bells are situated at St Mary-le-Bow church which is in the city of London which is E2, it's a beautiful iconic building which was rebuilt after the Great fire of London in 1666. The Bow Bells are perhaps the most famous ringers in the world and can be heard from a distance of six miles in Hackney. The area's most notable for being proper Cockney are Whitechapel, Bethnal Green, Spitalfields, Hoxton, Stepney, Limehouse, Poplar, Millwall, Hackney, Bow, Mile End, Bromley, Victoria Park and Isle of Dogs. Even if you're from Bermondsey you can qualify because it's said you can hear the church bells ring out South of the River Thames too.

They reckon that Cockney rhyming slang started around the 1840's because it was a bit of a code between the East End traders that the unsuspecting buyers weren't privy too then. Of course, the crafty Cockney could also use this slang and the nosey copper on the beat also wouldn't have a clue what was being exchanged. This was one of the reasons that inspector Frederick Abberline was posted into the East End because not only was he regarded as a fair copper to the East Enders, but he also spoke fluent Cockney and knew the area better than most. Often people complained that the other Coppers, apart from Abberline, were too heavy-handed but Frederick had the good folk of the East End's respect. I must say it's extremely impressive when you hear the Cockney speak in this unknown language and its only then you can appreciate just how much of a skill it would have been to know what one was saying in the moment. I'll list some prime example words below and you can try them for yourself and see if you could speak fluent East Ender:

SLANG	MEANING
Adam and Eve	Believe
Almond rocks	Socks
Apple fritter	Bitter (beer)
Apple peeling	Feeling
Apple tart	Heart
Apples and pears	Stairs
Aunty Lou	Flu
Barnet Fair	Hair
Beecham's pill	Hill
Bees' 'n' honey	Money

Bernard Miles	Piles (haemorrhoids)
Boat race	Face
Bo-peep	Sleep
Bottle and glass	Arse
Bow & arrow	Barrow
Box of toys	Noise
Brown bread	Dead
Bubble and squeak	Speak
Bunny	Talk (from rabbit and pork)
Burnt cinder	Window
Butcher's hook	Look
Can & Able	Table
Chalk Farm	Arm
Cherry-og	Dog
China plate	Mate (friend)
Coach 'n' badge	Cadge (get money off)
Cock 'n' hen	Ten or £10
Current bun	Sun
Derby Kelly	Belly
Dick Dirt	Shirt
Dig in the grave	Shave

Dr Crippen	Dripping
Dog and bone	Telephone
Donald Duck	Luck
Duke of Kent	Rent
First tuck	Luck
Frog and toad	Road
George Raft	Daft (crazy)
Ginger beer	Queer
Gold Watch	Scotch
Ham and eggs	Legs
Hamstead Heath	Teeth
Harry Lime	Time
Heap of coke	Bloke
Hen 'n' tox	Box
Holy frier	Liar
Holy ghost	Toast
House to let	Bet
Jack 'n' Jill	Till
Jam jar	Car
Jam tart	Heart
Jeremiah	Fire

Jim Skinner	Dinner
Joanna	Piano
Joe Blake	Steak
Kate Karney	Army
Lemon squash	Wash
Linen draper	Paper
Lots of bread	Head
Max Miller	Pillar
Mince pies	Eyes
Mother Hubbard	Cupboard
Mutt and Jeff	Deaf
Peckham Rye	Tie
Pig's ear	Beer
Plates of meat	Feet
Pork pie	Lie
Pot 'n' pan	Old man
Rabbit 'n' pork	Talk
Reads and writes	Fights
Reels of cotton	Rotten
Rocking horse	Sauce
Rory O'Moore	Floor

Rose Lee	Tea
Salmon and trout	Gout
Saucepan lid	Kid (child)
Sexton Blake	Cake
Joe Blake	Steak
Six to four	Whore
Skin 'n' blister	Sister
Skyrocket	Pocket
Taters in the mould	Cold
Tea leaf	Thief
Tit for tat	Hat
Tom and Dick	Sick
Trouble and strife	Wife
Mickey Duff	Puff/cannabis

Today the Cockney slang is still changing, and new words are being invented to be mixed into the street lingo. A proper Cockney is a certain type of Londoner known for ducking & diving, bobbing & weaving and wheeling & dealing his way through life to earn a pound note. The term mainly refers to speakers of the distinctive Cockney dialect of the English language, which is used in and around London, particularly by the working classes from the East End. Life for the Southern fairy is one hundred miles per hour compared to your Northern monkey! The Cockney has his/her own humour/craic, which to the average Northerner looking in seems like a foreign language, even though he/she only comes from 211 miles up the road in Manchester.

Where I grew up in Middlesbrough the delicacy the town raves about is the 'Parmo' which is basically chicken or pork in breadcrumbs, fried and topped with bechamel sauce and Cheddar cheese, the Teessider will go mad for it. In the East End its pie & mash, it goes back several decades, it's a Cockney tradition. The reason pie & mash is proper Cockney grub is that it was easy to make and filling. I mean for instance the potato's easy enough to come by, and if you went fishing in the Thames and caught enough eels then you could stick their meat in the pie after chopping the slippery things up. I'm told that the proper Cockney eats his pie & mash with a knife & spoon, not a knife and fork. Today, when these little traditional pie & mash shops in places such as Hoxton and Hackney do their pies, they're usually full of chicken, steak or mince, however the green liquor sauce, if it's done the traditional way is made using the water kept from the preparation of the stewed eels, however, many shops no longer use stewed eel water in their parsley liquor.

For over 94 years Tubby Isaacs ran a jellied eel stall in the East End, only closing as recently as 2013. Four generations of family sold fresh eels on Goulston Street (the street where Jack the Ripper dropped the rag and left his only clue), Brick Lane and Roman Road. A spokesman for the company said the extremely Cockney business closed because 'it was a sign of the times. It's truly heart-breaking because many of Tubby Isaac's customers had been loyal customers since the 1980's and many of Tubby Isaac's family members had worked for the business going as far back as the 1920's when it first opened. Many would say the secret to a good old bowl of jellied eels was in the cooking, the jelly exudes when the eels are boiled and it's that that creates a natural perseverative which can then be used for the next day.

The old Londoner didn't just feast on only eels, other things which could be fished out of the London River such as winkles, cockles and mussels were all on the menu in hard Victorian times when you needed to feed a family. Although I would never have had the balls to ever give jellied eels a go as to me it sounded as appealing as eating dog food, but I find it very sad that places such as Tubby Isaacs have vanished. For me, Tubby Isaacs is as much part of the Cockney culture as Jack the Ripper is.

Of course, back in the days of East End poverty, feeding the family eels was easy because the river Thames used to be crawling with them, at the time ringing up for a nice kebab wasn't an option, Just Eat didn't exist! If you wouldn't eat the eels, then you could have some fresh air pie and oxygen crisps for afters. All the men of the house had to do was cast their nets and they could feed their family and they were free, not to mention full of nutrition. One London favourite I did try however for the very first time was a bagel from the famous Brick Lane Bakery shop which never closes. I'd never tried a bagel in my entire life until I was 41.

Another thing the city of London has a link to is its very own gin. By the mid 1700's, Londoners were drinking, on average 112 pints of gin every year each. It was then, that the East End particularly was caught up in the gin craze that swept the whole of the city. Many East Enders would drink themselves to death on the stuff. For as little as a few pennies the good folk of the East End could escape their troubles for a few hours of not having to think about being hungry and having nowhere to go. This raw spirit would have such a hangover that often people refused to sober up and it was forever a vicious circle of drunkenness and bad behaviour which often led to them being arrested. Often you would see the advertising of these seedy gin shops who would promote things like, 'drunk for one penny, dead drunk for two and clean straw for nothing! The straw would be used the next day to sleep off the hangover.

"COCKNEY... AN AREA IN LONDON WHERE CRIMINALS LIVE."

ALAN PARTRIDGE

CHAPTER 4

GARY HUTTON - THE WHITECHAPEL HISTORIAN

I'm 54 years old and I was born in the Royal London Hospital in Whitechapel. I suppose that would make me as Cockney as they come. You don't have to be born in the East End to be a proper Cockney, you must be born within a square mile of a certain area which is called, 'the city'. To the East End of the city gates where the East End is and all the smelly industries. The West End of the city is where the posh people grew up. In the middle of both there's a church by St Paul's called, 'St Mary le-Bow. You must be born under the sound of the bells of that exact church to be a proper Cockney. Back in the day when there wasn't much traffic and not as many people you would hear the bells in Hampstead, North London. You could also hear them South of the river in Bermondsey so it's not just an East End thing being a Cockney. Often folk say, 'oh yeah I'm a Cockney' and where they were from there was no chance of them hearing those bells! A lot of people mistake the sound of the Bow Bells being from the area of Bow but it's not. There are two different places, there's the East End and then there's East London! The reality of it all is the East End is four postcodes which is E1, E2, E3 and E14 and the rest is East London. E4 for instance is out in Essex around Chingford way. E1 is Whitechapel/Aldgate, E2 is Bethnal Green/Bow and E3 is Limehouse/Isle of Dogs/Poplar E14 and that's where the real East End is. The East End is actually not that big! Often, I hear people saying I'm from the East End and they come from somewhere like Dagenham or Canning Town. Those places are not the East End, they're East London. Its two completely different places let me tell you! It's the River Lea that defines the East End. The East End starts from Aldgate, and it runs up towards the River Lea. In actual fact the river Lea is on the edge of Bow where the Bow Flyover is. The river Lea runs underneath that and looks like a little canal. The area Mile End is called Mile End because it is the first mile from the city gates. There were seven gates named Aldgate, Bishopsgate, Moorgate, Cripplegate, Aldersgate, Newgate and Ludgate. These were all gates that you paid taxes to go through so you could travel through the city, so Mile End Road was so named because that's where the first mile ended from Aldgate so the clues in the name of the place really!

Today I live out in Kent, but the East End is still very much in my heart. I'm actually CEO of a registered charity called 'Product of a Postcode' and I also wrote a book with that very same title as well. I believe that we're all products of a postcode and that our mentors and role models in early life make us what we grow up to be. If you have great mentors who are good influences in your life, then there's a good chance you're going to grow up and behave in life. If you've got bad one's like I had myself, and I was one of eleven children who had very little, then your start in life is going to be challenging.

My parents were Irish immigrants, and the East End was always a place where immigrants settled because it was cheap. My parents settled in Brick Lane in the 1950's then had eleven children. Although times were hard, I had a lovely life and was washed, clothed, schooled, took to church and fed by Catholic nuns. When my youngest sibling was 18 months old, the oldest was 15. When I was 7 my mother sadly died of Leukaemia and the nuns told me my old lady had gone to live in Heaven with Jesus. Of course, I didn't understand, and I wanted to go live with her and Jesus because the nuns told me what an amazing place it all is up there. Not long after mam died my life turned around 360-degrees. My old man was an alcoholic who was working in

Trueman's Brewery on Brick Lane. These smelly industries were what East London was all about and because there were so many warehouses on the manor, it was then, at such a young age, that I learnt to shoplift. The first time I was ever arrested by the Old Bill I was only 9. All of my mentors at that time went out to earn a pound note in a boiler suit and balaclava. I started doing bits and bobs with them from my early teen years and that made me think, 'God I want to be like you guys when I'm older!' From such a young age I was introduced to a life of crime just so we could eat as a family!

Where I grew up on the edge of the city, you could see the tall buildings of London, but nobody aspired to go work in them! I never knew anyone who went out at 7am and came home at 5pm to sit around their table to talk about their day at work. Nothing like that happened in my life because everyone I knew was 'at it' and that's maybe why I grew up and ended up on the front page of The News of the World paper for being part of a group which flooded Great Britain with counterfeit money. One day I ended up in a strait jacket and in a padded cell whilst being pumped with drugs.

At one point in my life, I thought it was macho to be in prison and beat paedophiles and rapists up. I guess my sub-conscious was hiding something from me, that's when I went on a journey of self-discovery and only then did I find out who Gary Vincent Hutton really was. That's when I changed my ways, wrote a book and decided I wanted to help people in life. I have two organisations called, 'Product of a Postcode' and 'London Giving'. I go around to the homeless and provide food, clothing and just somebody to talk to. Myself and my guys go all over the East and West End's where the homeless congregate. We've also now got a team called 'Nottingham Giving' which are out in their own city doing the same as we do in London. These are people made up of volunteers who spend their weekends helping these people in great need. My group have been putting things up on an Amazon Wishlist for the items needed for the homeless and then the kind people donate to what we've asked for, things such as sleeping bags, hats and gloves. When we've accumulated enough stuff, we go on the streets with hot food and make their lives better because of people's kind donations. I'm just hoping through this book that my registered charities can get some well-earned attention.

Growing up around Brick Lane and Whitechapel as a whole I was very familiar with the names of Jack the Ripper and Reggie & Ronnie Kray, but they never meant anything to me. They may do to people up North but on my manor, there was loads of these well-known criminal names such as Jack "spot" Comer and the Dixon brothers, George and Alan. To tell you the truth when I was growing up, we were more familiar with the name Jack the Ripper because often parents would tell their children that they needed to be in at a certain time or 'Jack will get you'. In all honesty, the people in the East End don't subscribe to this hero-worshipping of the likes of the Kray twins, Lenny McLean, Roy Shaw or other East End villains like some do up North. No one from my area gets it and neither do I and I'll tell you why, I personally know members of some of the victims' families who were hurt or killed. When I see these charity gatherings in places such as The Blind Beggar on Whitechapel Road, I don't get it, I mean, come on that's a murder scene! People are glorifying it and I can't go along with that! If you come from where I'm from then you understand all of this glamourising crime nonsense, but I'm not going to party where a family member of someone I know was shot through the head. It may all look cool and fantastic to the people in Newcastle, Glasgow and Aberdeen but not from where I come from it's not! To us lot growing up on our manor then it was just two snappy-dressing blokes from Vallance Road who owned the local snooker hall. If you went around the corner from Ronnie & Reggie Kray, then you would bump into another 'bad un' doing something criminal but completely different! All the tasty geezers in the East End were going out and getting a pound note and didn't seek the PR that the Krays so badly wanted and eventually that was their downfall. The Krays were not even really active criminals themselves, what they would do was wait until someone had something away and then they'd march in and steal it from them taking their wack. The victim couldn't go to the Old Bill because he'd stolen it in the first place, and also if he did then that person would be known as a 'grass' and it would be a death sentence for him in his own community. Those two were better known as 'thieves ponce's' back in the day. People think because the Krays were from Bethnal Green that they did all their graft there but there wasn't anything at Bethnal Green at that time. All the illegal spielers were in Whitechapel then. Those two were basically leeches and that's how they made a living. For people to worship the likes of those two I think is wrong.

Today in 2022 I often go into schools and prisons and tell the young people that looking up to the likes of the twins is all wrong. When I go into places such as Feltham jail which hosts hundreds of these lost youths, I tell them the importance of education in the youth. A lot of these kids today think it's cool to be involved with gang culture which doesn't even really exist. The reality is it's just a group of mates who are all out committing low-level street crime. For hundreds of years that anti-social conduct has always happened. Forever since day dot in the East End there's always been a group of scallywags out on the rob to try and get a few quid, very much like the Artful Dodger and his boys in Oliver Twist.

I'm a motivational speaker and when I have three-hundred people in one room and I say the word 'gangs', automatically they get a picture of a young black kid, face covered and trying to look extra bad. I never give them that picture, the media have given them that image. Through the 1970s we were told that type of person was a mugger, then through the 1980s/90s this person was a rapist, but you can't call them that no more so let's just call them gangs! That is stereo-typical racism. When I go into places such as Pentonville prison and tell them things like that they frown.

I had one young boy who I was working with, and I asked him what he did each time he came out. He told me that he couldn't go back to where he lived because he was gang affiliated. I asked him what that really meant, which made me come across as a bit stupid to him no doubt. He told me that him and his pals get a narcotic product, and they'll all sell it for a share of the profits. When I asked him if he had to 'pay up' he didn't have a clue what I was on about! I asked him if he had to pay people for what he did and he said no, then I told him he wasn't in a gang then and that the only gang in the world was the New York mafia and that you had to pay up. The geezer who sits at the top of that mob is called the 'gang star' or the 'godfather' and not only do you have to pay up to him, but you have to go out and work for him and do what he says you do, otherwise bad things will happen to you and your family. I told him that he actually wasn't even in a gang and it was all bollocks.

When I was growing up in the East End through the 1970s it wasn't like it is now, with the streets all tidied and lit up. In my youth the whole of the East End was a very dark, dingy and an unkempt place. Also, there were still prostitutes on many of the street corners. You would see the working girls plying their trade on the manor every night until around the turn of the millennium. These days they're all gone, however, if you walk around places such as Vallance Road near the bridge of Cheshire Street in the early hours you'll still see the odd one. Most of them moved on over to Hackney and different parts of London.

When I was a kid Spitalfields Market was incredibly busy with lorry drivers, and that's who would give the sex workers their custom. I often would see the brasses fighting with their pimps, dodgy customers and even each other over being territorial of their patch.

I know over the years people have been outspoken, about how many different cultures are settling in Whitechapel but for as long as I can remember, Whitechapel has always been full of immigrants who've settled here, worked hard and built up a good living and moved their families out. I don't remember Whitechapel being any different to how it is now. These immigrants settled in Whitechapel because it was a cheap area with lots of industries. Many of the real Londoners just refused to work because they chose a life of crime, so when the immigrants rolled their sleeves up and put a graft in like an eager beaver then good on them. Also, the rag trade (making clothes) was very prominent so if you could use a sewing machine then you were going to find work all day long. Many of the top high street clothing stores in London were all made in the East End back in the day. So many businesses of this nature were set up around Petticoat and Brick Lane's and went on to establish themselves so they could all feed their families. That's the real reason why there's so many different cultures in Whitechapel. For decades upon decades immigrants have settled such as

Jewish, Irish, Bangladesh, Pakistan and West Indies and that makes the place what it is today. Today I'm in my early 50's but I'm still as passionate as ever about the East End, particularly Whitechapel obviously because it's the place of my birth. On Facebook I've got two groups, one being 'Whitechapel born n bred' and also 'I was born in the East End, not East London' and I regularly put up all the old history bits and pieces on those for the growing following I have.

I relax by studying history and helping people. When I say the history of Whitechapel, I won't go deep into Jack the Ripper like most do simply because I'm bored of it. Us folk from Whitechapel have heard every story there is to be told about him. There's so much history from our area other than a knife-wielding maniac who nobody knows who he was. All you get asked if you're from our area of London is Jack the Ripper questions but I'm going to give you a few examples of other interesting faces from Whitechapel. Joseph Merrick aka 'The Elephant Man' lived in Whitechapel Hospital. Vidal Sassoon CBE the very famous hairdresser, he's probably the most famous hairdresser in the world but he started off on Whitechapel Road doing an apprenticeship as a boy. Vidal Sassoon products are sold right across the world today in 2022 and that guy started off in Whitechapel. Although he died in 2012, he's still got salons across the West End of London with his name above the door. The church hymn 'Amazing Grace' was written by John Newton, and he was from Whitechapel. John's mother died when he was extremely young and his father didn't know what to do with him, so they put him in a boarding school. When his old man then met a woman in Essex, he just kept John in the boarding school to be brought up. When John left there, he went and travelled on slave ships. When he saved up enough money, he bought his own ship and became an incredibly wealthy man. On one of his ships journeys the sea became so brutal to the point that he got on his knees during the storm and asked for grace. Eventually, the storm calmed and when he got back to England he left the shipping industry, wrote Amazing Grace and became a minister in a church. He then spent his whole life preaching the word of the lord from the good book. The old comedy double act Flanagan and Allen were from Hanbury Street (where Jack the Ripper killed Annie Chapman) just off Brick Lane. One of the most famous people ever to come out of this area is the singer Billy Ocean. I've known Billy all my life and although he was born in Trinidad and Tobago, his family settled in Whitechapel. Billy started off in the tailoring industry but when he bought an old piano and started writing songs, he then took off bigtime. Billy has now become a multi-million selling artist and has done very well for himself.

Going back to my childhood through the 1970s, when these groups of Jack the Ripper tours came around our manor, myself and my gang would often terrorise the tourists. I would see them walking around Hanbury and Durward Streets and I knew that these 'out of towners' would be there for the taking and some of them got robbed. We never ever felt bad about it because these people were coming to our area to glamourise five girls being murdered once upon a time. I found it quite insulting if I'm honest and that's why so many of them got done over. In the summer there would be hundreds of tourists walking around Aldgate, Whitechapel and Spitalfields all obsessed over Jack the bloody Ripper and I used to think, 'what the fuck is going on?!' As the years have gone on the groups have gotten smaller, although there seems to be more of these little groups of people all walking around listening to some guide telling them about women having their throats cut and being disembowelled.

If you google how many football teams there are in London it will tell you thirteen. It also says there are three East End clubs which it lists as West Ham, Leyton Orient and Dagenham & Redbridge but that's not true. There actually aren't any teams from the East End, only East London. The only true East End club, and I hate to admit this, is Millwall because they used to be located under E14 which was the Isle of dogs Canary Wharf which was the docks area and a little bit of it is called Millwall. Millwall Football Club originally started up there for the dock workers in 1885. It was only after they grew as a club that they moved across to South London and settled there so really, it's an East End club. West Ham United came from the ironworks under E16 and that's why they get the nickname, 'The Hammers'. Leyton Orient really is East London on the other side of Hackney so today there really is no true East End football team. People from the East End just gravitated to West Ham. The Hammers have a huge following now out in Essex way because when they knocked down all of the slums, everyone from the East End moved out to Essex and people from South London i.e., Bermondsey, they shipped out to Kent. The reason I personally moved out over to Kent was because I didn't want to keep bumping into all the old faces from the East End and I knew they'd all be in Essex.

If you want my honest opinion of where the heart of the East End is I would have to say it's what was Stepney. Stepney doesn't exist anymore, but it was a London Borough, but they emulated it into Tower Hamlet. Stepney for me was the heart of the East End. The real East End of London is disappearing really fast. With the dynamics and diversity of people turning up on the manor now and all the different religions of the world, the old East End pub culture is no longer existent.

Today in 2022 it's all become so expensive, and most people can only afford to come into the area if they're wealthy or their parents are. I do think it's great for the area that all these new plush apartments and high story buildings are going up, however, it's for all these young clubbers who are coming into the estate. All the young mob are doing what they do and it's building up the drug economy at the same time. I have to say the narcotic problem in the East End is as bad as it's ever been. For instance, I've walked along Brick Lane and dealers have come up to me and have given me their business card which say, 'phone me for gear' on it! I said to him, 'I could have been Old Bill for all you know and arrested you on the spot', he just looked at me with a puzzled look and said, "ooh, I didn't think of that"! That's just one example of how the manor is rife with drugs. Back in my day these young lads weren't into drugs because they were into boxing gyms.

The East End has always had a huge influx of boxing gyms scattered all over because it's the East End's way. Boxing was an escape from the concrete jungle for these wayward boys. It put discipline into lads who greatly needed it and I dare say it saved lots of East Enders.

Although being involved in things such as boxing clubs as a boy like I was briefly, some of us are destined to end up in jail. It's very sad that so many people from our part of the London will eventually go to prison, that's why it's invaluable that these kids find their passion in early life and channel it in the correct manner. If they do that then there's a better chance these youngsters won't be going to the big house. Over the years I've spoken with these kids I work with and when they've been sent to work in a warehouse they've lasted six weeks, now if that kid's passion is writing, painting or singing then they'd be prepared to do that for free until it paid off. It may take them to write one-hundred books to succeed but whilst doing that, they're not out robbing people, smoking dope or drinking on street corners. You must find your passion from a young age, whether that be boxing, football or acting then you must focus on that path. Like anything in life, if you're going to succeed at it then you must be consistent, hard-working and prolific, but if you do something you love then you're developing a true passion.

One of my best mates is ex-ABA Lightweight champion from the Repton ABC, Tony Cesay, he was the captain of the club, and I grew up with him. I used to play football with Tony as a kid and he was very good, but he hurt his ankle and that's when he went to the Repton and it's probably the best decision he ever made. Tony, through boxing, travelled the world with the club, won championships and became a somebody. Today he's still involved in training people and boxing has giving him a full life of doing what he's doing. Tony is a prime example of how boxing has saved someone and there's many others from our manor that it's also done the same for.

The Repton Amateur Boxing Club for example has done such an amazing job because if you show an interest, they'll help you along in life, and in more ways than just the boxing. If you turn up all the time and behave in the gym, then people such as the chairman Davey Robinson who ran his own stonemason business would give you a job. Tony Burns (R.I.P) did this also with so many of the kids that came through their doors. The Repton is more than just a boxing gym, it's like you're joining a big family when you sign up.

S&R Kelly & Sons on Bethnal Green Road does the greatest pie & mash in the world. That little gaff at the top of Vallance Road selling the Londoner's favourite grub will be there forever. It's the same a little further on down the road at Pellicci's. I used to go to Nevio Pellicci's place every single morning through the 80s for my breakfast.

Just off Brick Lane used to be a whole estate called Flower & Dean Street and it was one of the roughest places in the whole of Great Britain. Of course, it's long gone now but as a kid, I can't remember that street being up before it was ripped down. The geezer who invented the Harlem Globetrotters American basketball team came out of Flower & Dean Street. A world famous but a small (5ft 3 inches) Yiddish fella named Abe Saperstein from the East End all started that. If you've heard the expression, 'being on tenterhooks" that comes from our manor also. When the silk-weavers who settled on Brick Lane would put their bits of silk out to dry in the sun they would put it on this drying surface called a tenter, this had hooks on each side so it would stretch out, that's where that saying comes from. In fact, there's a Street in Whitechapel named Tenter Street. On the edge of the city, you've got a place called Houndsditch which is on the border of the city and the East End. The reason it's called Houndsditch is because when people's dogs died, they'd walk over to this place and chuck their dead mutt in the ditch. The name Whitechapel comes from a church which was on Whitechapel Road, it was damaged during World War 2 so now these days it's a park. When this church was still up, inside there was a little white chapel and that's where the name for our manor comes from.

If someone asks me where I'm from I tell them with pride I'm from the East End and I'm telling the truth because I'm from Whitechapel. You get people out there saying they're from the East End and when I ask them where, they've said, "Barking" and I just laugh. The correct term for one of those types is 'mockneys' because they're just fake Cockneys! Those breeds always overdramatise things like in that show, The Only Way Is Essex. The way they speak and walk around saying things like, "SHAAT UP" and other things like, "OOH MY GOD" etc blah blah blah... It's just not how proper Londoners speak and it's a bit insulting! People from East London speak totally different to us lot from the East End.

The East End of London is unique in so many different ways from the other parts of London. If you google my name today one of the first things that comes up apart from the counterfeit job is the famous joke that East Ender Micky Flanagan tells. I'll let you all Google it now so you can find out the rest (laughs).

I think before the East End becomes too unrecognisable, everyone should go out and walk around the East End just one more time. If you'd like to contact me for any projects or enquiries, then please get in touch by the following –

EMAIL – productofapostcode@yahoo.com

YOUTUBE – Product of a postcode TV

INSTAGRAM – mr.product_of_a_postcode

FACEBOOK – 'I Grew Up in The Eastend Not Whitechapel' & 'Whitechapel born n bred'

TWITTER – Product of A Postcode

"It's good they're holding the Olympics in the East End of London. Means the athletes will have to use extra skill to work out which gunshots is the starting pistol."

Frankie Boyle 2012

CHAPTER 5
MICK P. PRIESTLEY – JACK THE RIPPER EXPERT/AUTHOR/TOUR GUIDE

Today I live in Whitechapel, but I originate from Sunderland in the Northeast. I first moved to London when I was 21 almost twenty years ago and I started off in Camden. I was a guitarist in a band and music is really why I came to the bright lights of London in the first place. I wouldn't move to Whitechapel until I'd already been in the capital for a decade or so, but I'd always been fascinated with true crime, so I was very well aware of Whitechapel for obvious reasons.

Before I became a tour guide on Jack and taking groups around the city, I decided I was going to write a book on him. Through my research for Jack the Ripper I linked in with a few people within the Jack the Ripper circle, one of those being my boss, Richard Cobb from the tour guides who would go on to employ me. Richard incidentally wrote a book about another Ripper but the one from Yorkshire and it's him who runs the tour guide. To cut a long story short that's how I am where I am today walking around the streets of Whitechapel with groups of captivated people wanting to know all about the Whitechapel fiend.

Getting involved with the Jack the Ripper walks was great for me because I have a memory like a sponge, particularly if it's something I'm interested in such as the Whitechapel killings. To be familiar with the times, dates and places of 1888's events became second nature to me whether I was sitting in the archives writing my book, 'One Autumn in Whitechapel' or I was learning to become a professional tour guide. Over the years I've become grossly interested in the whole East End/Jack the Ripper case to the point I now have encyclopaedia knowledge of it all. Jack the Ripper has now become a huge part of my life, from writing the book, to what I do at work every single day and also living on his old manor. Even if I'm not at work, I'm that well known now in Whitechapel that random people come up to me in the street to ask me my thoughts on the case!

There's a saying in life that goes, 'if you enjoy what you're doing then you'll never work a day in your life', well I talk about the autumn of terror from 1888 every single day so I can very much relate to that quote. If I was working somewhere else on a different job, I'd probably be talking about Jack the Ripper and not getting paid for it. I usually work 5/6 days a week doing the tours at various parts of the day in groups as big as up to forty strong. That may sound daunting but it's fantastic once I get going. My tours usually last around one hour forty-five minutes and they usually start at 7.30 pm and finish around 9.15 pm. It isn't only Joe public off the estates who've come on my tours, I've taken around some very famous celebrities such as film star Charlie Sheen, TV personality Kelly Osbourne and rock star Vinnie Paul. A few of my colleagues have also taken around some very famous names such as Simon Cowell, one of the guys from One Direction and Russell Brand. More often than not there's always a well-known face who will turn up to hear everything about saucy Jack's handy work. On a typical tour, there are also people from every corner of the world such as Germany, America, Australia, China and Japan etc... The folk have all heard of this mysterious villain named Jack and all are intrigued to want to learn more, so they book up with me and my tour.

Although we don't even know who this Jack the Ripper was, it seems that everywhere in the world has heard of him, even if they don't know the full story and he's just a name at that point.

Often people will come and book up for a stag/hen do, 40th birthday party or even just the local Christmas office party from work. Although I'm technically classed as a Mackem (Sunderland person), I've lived in London for most of my adult life so that must mean I'm some kind of adopted Cockney because I emigrated to London. Today in 2022 I've become used to the busyness the city brings and because I'm so gripped with London's history, which is on every corner, then it's a place I never grow tired of. The great city of London and all its historic importance is very much my kind of place! If ever I get the train back to Sunderland, I find it's like the world has slowed down because the North is so much slower than Whitechapel. If any of my Northern friends come to visit me in London then they say the opposite of, 'oh it's far too busy down here' and that, 'everyone is in such a hurry' blah blah blah.

Although I've now been in London for such a long time there's still so much to learn. Referring to another famous quote said by Samuel Johnson that goes, "when a man is tired of London, he is tired of life" he also followed it up by saying something along the lines of, 'because of all the little back alleys in the city, you could live ten lives and not see all of London' and I fully get his point. Another factor which always reels me in about Whitechapel is that during the blitz in the second World War, along with Bethnal Green this is where the main action was. Where Bethnal Green library is today was one of the first buildings to be hit and it must have been so frightening to witness those German planes flying so low and firing at the area. For instance, when I'm on my walking tours in Spitalfields there are rows of houses from the 18th century, then all of a sudden, you'll see houses from the 1950s, that's an example of the rebuilding that happened after WW2 in the East End. I'd still say about 25% of the manor hasn't changed since the Victorian times.

As I walk around the East End there are so many other things to learn about the area and I'm not talking about things just to do with the blitz, the Krays or Jack the Ripper, I mean, for the past 1000 years the East End is the place where every notable person has come to.

I have written two books on Jack the Ripper. The first is a guidebook called, 'Jack the Ripper – The essential Visitors Guide'. I sell the 32-page book on my tour which is a souvenir, but my real piece of art is my main one, 'Jack the Ripper – One Autumn in Whitechapel' I put my heart and soul into that book. The new book I'm writing is called, 'Active Shooter' which is another true crime one about an American shooting case in a shopping mall.

When I'm at work, most days there's always something going on in Whitechapel, for instance only the other day I was walking along Brick Lane and these guys came out trying to sell me a curry but someone from another shop said, "oh this is Mick and he's the local Ripper man" so we kind of all know each other in the community.

Whenever people talk about the legendary happenings in the old East End, they're usually bad things i.e., Jack the Ripper, the Krays, bombings, the Black Death or other East End villains such as Jack Spot but that's what people are interested in. For example, take the Tower of London. The only reason that all these tourists go there is because of all the acts of brutality which have happened there. So, when you're walking around the East End and think well, this is where the Great Train Robbers are from etc... You wouldn't walk around with a great big grin on your face, but it totally captivates people. Particularly if these cases are so old and everyone who've been involved are now long gone. The Tower of London for instance has got hundreds and hundreds of years of history and inside there people will have been hung, drawn and quartered for fun. If you love this type of dark history, then there's no place on earth better than the East End of London. I just don't get the same buzz that I do when I'm walking around North, South or West London as I do with the East. For instance, most of the history in the West End is more recent things, such as The Beatles or Jimi Hendrix, but there's far less darkness, blood and guts than the East End.

For all the years I've now been living in London I've never had any trouble. I can say Whitechapel has been very good to me. People say often that the East End is the roughest but it's where I feel the safest in the whole of the city. Yes, I know the East End has its fair share of homeless beggars and druggies, but I think I know just about everyone now.

If I'm ever in the Ten Bells pub in Spitalfields I can't stop myself from running things through in my mind of yesteryear events like it being where Annie Chapman (Dark Annie) popped her head through the door before she was killed or just outside of it was Mary Jane Kelly's patch to hook a punter. I still sometimes look up at Christ Church next door or look over to where Dorset Street (a street once so scary that Victorian police would only go down in fours) once was and I never tire of it. It doesn't ever get old! People often ask the question, 'Mick don't you get bored of doing the same Jack the Ripper walk ever day?' The answer is simply no. I know there's a whole new bunch of people to come along and all are as interested as the previous lot who've paid their hard-earned money and it's a subject which will continue to fascinate me until the day I die.

If somebody put a gun to my head and said, 'tell me who you think was Jack the Ripper' I'd have to say that it was Albert Bachert. Bachert was the chairman of the Vigilance Committee and although his parents were German, he was raised in

Whitechapel and lived fully in the murder zone when they were happening. He also fits the correct description from witness statements and is the perfect age. If you spoke to a psychologist today than they would tell you the murderer would have had a criminal record exactly like Bachert's. He would often inject himself into the investigation and even told the police he'd met the killer and said he'd spoke to him on a couple of occasions. He also said the killer was writing letters to his home to threaten him and warn him of more murders. He said Jack had even chalked words on his house, but it was washed away before the police saw it. He turned up uninvited at the inquest of Francis Coles murder in February 1891 at the Working Lad's Institute on Whitechapel Road demanding to be on the jury so that he could see the body in the mortuary at Old Montague Street nearby. When the coroner told him he wouldn't be allowed in it was then he caused such a big scene to the point he was threatened with being removed from the building. That sounds like he just wanted to see the body one last time on the morgue slab. Bachert's job was that he engraved things and the reason that's interesting is there was a number of women in the Whitechapel area who had met an individual who must have been the killer because he'd tried to attack them, just like the women who'd survived Ted Bundy and Peter Sutcliffe a century or so later. When these ladies spoke after surviving Jack's onslaught, they all said that after meeting him in the Spitalfields/Whitechapel area, the one thing he'd done before attacking them was give them dud highly polished brass coins. They were purposely machined around the edges so that they'd pass off as half-crowns. That was the Victorian equivalent of a dodgy £50 note. The Met and City police had teams of detectives looking for men who'd been ripping off prostitutes with fake coins and that was very much what the killer had been doing but many Ripperologists have forgotten about that story, and it's rarely brought up. In 1889 Albert Bachert was arrested and taken to court for two separate incidents of passing on counterfeit coins exactly the same as what the alleged killer had been doing in a number of pubs. From all my research into the case I'm convinced Albert Bachert was our man. Someone would have to come along and show me a whole new suspect to change my mind of who Jack the Ripper really was! If today there was a load of brutal slayings all over Whitechapel, then Scotland Yard's No.1 guy brought in would be Albert Bachert in my opinion. I think in Victorian times most people tied to the case must have thought Bachert was a constant nuisance but because of that he wasn't suspected as a serial killer. He's certainly forgotten about over today's leading suspects such as Aaron Kosminski, Montague Druitt, Michael Ostrog, Francis Tumblety, George Chapman, Charles Cross (Lechmere) and James Maybrick etc... At the time, apart from John Pizer (leather apron) there was hardly any suspects, now 134 years later there's hundreds of the buggers and it's all come about since Stephen Knights Royal philosophy from the 1970s almost a century later.

It does get annoying when I hear people say, 'the killer was one of the Royal Family' with a straight face. In fact, Prince Albert Victor or 'Eddy' had an alibi for four of the five murders and wasn't even in the country on the nights in question.

Quite recently I was talking to someone in Waterstones and they confirmed to me that Stephen Knight's book, 'Jack the Ripper – The Final Solution' is the greatest selling book of all on Jack, although most ripper experts acknowledge it as complete nonsense, however it sells greatly so outlets are happy to stock it and pass on more tall stories regarding Jack.

It's alleged that years later Stephen Knight even said he made it all up, but it was a cracking story none the less. Many of these theories are truly outstanding for films and books but there was never any substance at the time I can assure you readers. Not so much Aaron Kosminski because he was mentioned at the time but most of the alleged serious suspects today are only there on merit because these authors of the many books are trying to add weight to their theory which of course really is to make money to sell their books. Many of these top authors don't really understand true crime or they simply can't be bothered to sit in the archives for years on end doing the correct detective work which is required for such a unique case. Of course, these authors are never going to say, 'well in actual fact my guy never did it but it's a good story'! No, they want you all to think they've finally cracked the case and you must read the book now!

Usually when you buy a book about a serial killer then it's by somebody who understands true crime such as an ex-detective. Say for instance if someone wrote something on the Yorkshire Ripper case then because it's so recent, you would then have relatives coming forward and saying, 'well that's not quite right' but because everyone is dead connected with the Whitechapel case of 1888, then these authors can say what they want, and nobody will question them. That's why so many of the 200 plus books on Jack are extremely thin on the sufficient details. It's my opinion that several of these titles are conning the unknowing public because they don't know any different. It's only the real experts such as the Richard Jones, Martin Fido (R.I.P), Donald Rumbelow, Paul Begg or Stewart Even's of this world that would say, 'well hang on a minute that's not quite right'!

The reason these people can get away with it for so long is all the physical evidence which once existed in Scotland Yard is long gone and nobody can say any different. (Author's note – Much of the evidence from 1888 was destroyed during the WW2 Blitz and what we do know about the case comes from old newspapers) It's largely known that many that write the books are getting their information from yesteryears newspapers. To do a valid account and do the story justice it would take one of these authors years of going through the archives. The rumours that Scotland Yard have secret draws full of physical evidence on the case are very far off the mark regarding the case.

If you'd like to get in touch with Mick, then you can contact him at the following –

INSTAGRAM - @mppriestley

EMAIL – hello@ripperworld.net or thejacktherippertour.com

My book is extremely graphic. I make no apologies for it. But it is graphic only because I told the truth about what the Ripper did to his victims.

Bernard Schaffer, Whitechapel – The Final Stand of Sherlock Holmes

CHAPTER 6
THE ART OF PUGILISM & EAST END VILLIANY

The earliest evidence of boxing dates back to Egypt around 3000 BC, however if you ask me, the home of real pugilism is the York Hall on Old Ford Road in the East End of London. Even the voice of British boxing Steve Bunce says the mecca of world boxing isn't Madison Square Garden like many would think, it's in Bethnal Green. All three Kray brothers Charlie, Ronnie and Reggie would all grace that famous hall with their pugilistic skills and then walk around the corner back home to Vallance Road.

The reason why everyone wanted to box growing up in the East End is that their fathers and grandfathers went before them. Reggie Kray once said that it was commonplace that the men in the East End on one hand would be more for their mothers in a loving way but wanted to be fighters like their fathers on the other hand. Most Cockney youths grew up on dad's or granddads boxing booth stories on Bethnal Green Road or Barnet Fair.

The noble art of boxing has been linked to the East End since the sport was invented. When growing up in poverty and having nothing, it was often that whoever punched the hardest in the street got what he wanted and that was life. Fundamentally if one was going to choose to be a professional criminal in life, they would at least learn the basics of pugilism.

Whitechapel godfather Jack 'spot' Comer only ever mastered the very basics of boxing yet moulded them into his own style for his particular chosen craft of becoming a professional criminal. He didn't need to learn the art of slipping and feints when he and his gang would be circling you like wolves and kicking the living daylights out of you in numbers, there was no sportsmanship needed in their eyes. In that gangster world there was never going to be any Lord Marquess of Queensbury rules.

Jewish Jack Spot's gang were called "The Yiddishers" and his comrades such as Morris Goldstein aka "Moisha Blueball" and Bernard Schack aka "Sonny the Yank" ran the protection rackets of Whitechapel in the 1930's. It was Spot & Co that opposed the growing fascist movement and attacked members of the British Union of Fascists led by Sir Oswald Mosley, later known as the Battle of Cable Street in the autumn of 1936.

Regardless of any decade, London has always had a gang problem, even from less well-known names than the Krays, Richardsons and Nashs such as the Hoxton, Aldgate, Elephant & Castle, Islington mobs. Other dangerous gangs in London in the same period were The Sabini's (Italian heritage), Russian Jews Bessarabian Tigers, Camden Town's Broad mob, King's Cross Gang, Odessians and The West End Boys. If you look at all the vicious London notorious gangsters that have become infamous such as Tony Mella, Billy Hill, Ronnie & Reggie Kray, Freddie Foreman, Joey Pyle etc all would take boxing training early on in life to help them go on to become what they went on to become.

Few can argue that so many top fighters were born within ear shot of the Bow Bells than any other part of the country. If you look at every part of the real East End, then history runs deep with champion after champion from the elite level production line of special fighters. Who can remember that little shop on Bethnal Green Road ran by ex-flyweight champ Charlie Magri? Every amateur, professional or aspiring fighter would make a play for at least buying one thing from there at least once in their life, just so they could carry the flash plastic bag around. Young lads would carry them bags with pride. It was very much a sign of, 'yeah look at me, I'm a fighter'!

In 1787 Daniel Mendoza, the first ever bareknuckle champion came from Bethnal Green. There were no Queensbury rules in those days and fighters only knew how to come forward and throw haymakers, with each punch possibly not only ending your career but your life. The fighting prowess was there then but eye-catching style and grace for the fighter from the East End was yet to come. Many a fighter from that time would fight under the influence of drink for Dutch courage which was usually cheap gin. Moving on a bit to the 1920's, Aldgate's Ted 'kid' Lewis had refined Cockney brawling skills winning titles galore as a featherweight. Another featherweight in the 1960's Terry Spinks was the new face in the boxing world after turning pro from having 200 amateur bouts. That glittering amateur career saw him become the youngest ever boxer to win Olympic Gold in 1956. Terry Spinks' life was a real rag to riches story considering he was only working as a binman before that gold medal. Terry boxed for the very famous West Ham Boys Club which many years later the dynamite banger Nigel Benn would win the ABA title for. Today Nigel Benn holds, still to this day, some records for tv viewing figures of his fights. His legacy is perhaps the last link to the unique world that existed pre-war Newham, Tower, Hamlets, Hackney, Barking and Ilford which bred a working-class fighting spirit that produced champion after champion.

Some of the quaint historic signposts of East End boxing still stand today. West Ham Baths was a well-known local boxing venue for watching amateur or professional boxing all night. Until the 1980's the London Borough of Newham was one of the few places to still have Victorian bath houses where members of the public, without such private amenities, could wash. These bath houses on Romford Road were later converted into the current Newham Leisure Centre. Newham Boys amateur boxing club in Church Street, Stratford also emerged from a bath house during the 1980's and the original architecture still remains.

The nation's oldest boxing gym is the Repton and the one I'm most familiar with. Tucked away from Brick Lane, The Repton has the rep of the toughest place in London and has been used for various filming, from Lock, Stock & Two Smoking Barrels, to music videos from Take That. The club is very different from a lot of 'keep fitters' in the area as it has a strict code of, 'boxers only'! The club doesn't go commercial if they can help it and the club's motto of, "NO GUTS... NO GLORY" is a very fitting one at that. Every time I'm in London I always make a point of popping in to see 'Diamond' Davey Robinson who's the chairman of the Bethnal Green club. Davey's the longest serving chairman of any boxing club in Great Britain today, he took the role in the mid-1970s. The gym was established in 1884 and a few of their famous fighters consist of John H Stracey, Ronnie & Reggie Kray (we know what they went on to become, but they started here) Actor and East End boy done good Ray Winstone, Maurice Hope, Olympian winner Audley Harrison, Andy Lee and former world middleweight champion Darren Barker. The gym's address still remains Repton Boxing Club, The Bath House, Cheshire Street London E2 to this day. This underscores the architecture, amenities and social-economic realities of London's poorest communities from the Victorian age and the enduring link to the fight game. Gangsters, criminals and thieves trained alongside 'straight goers' and it didn't matter from which walk of life they came from they had boxing in common. Rocky Marciano and Sonny Liston had their ties with naughty people no matter how much they tried to distance their names from them and that's how it is with gangsters and the sport of boxing in the tough East

End of London. It is a 'dog-eat-dog' world and only the fittest will survive.

"When I stopped boxing that's when I started getting my left-hook together more, and that played a great part in my street fights."

Reg Kray 2000

CHAPTER 7
THE MURDER SPOTS TODAY IN 2022

You've read about how the residents aren't happy with Whitechapel being connected to the world's most infamous serial killer, and when you walk around the manor these days you can see the authorities have done their best to change how Whitechapel is perceived. I hope I don't offend you Whitechapel lot by saying the only reason I even knew where Whitechapel was, was because of the murders.

When I walk around the murder spots where these poor girls were butchered you really have to use your imagination to go back in time to 1888. The first murder scene is Bucks Row (now Durward Street), and for me this has the least amount of aura about it, mainly because it's changed so much. On that Friday, August 31st Jack the Ripper took his first victim, Mary 'Polly' Nichols, just behind Whitechapel High Street before disappearing into the dark streets of London. For the last five years or so, the murder spot was closed off to the public, so it was impossible to get nearby. That all changed in August 2021 when Whitechapel Underground Station re-opened, and the spot where Mary Nichols was found at 3:40am is directly where the entrance is. At first, she was mistaken for a random drunk or a bundle of rags, but sadly she was neither of those things. If Polly was murdered today in that very same spot, then you would have to step over her body to get into the Tube Station. Today, as the thousands of people walk past the brand-new entrance of the Whitechapel tube station, I do wonder if anyone stops and pauses for one moment and thinks about her and what that wicked killer did to her that night.

The second of the five locations is Hanbury Street where Annie Chapman was murdered. Annie's mutilated body was found in the backyard of 29 Hanbury Street. The full row of terraced houses is now long gone as they were demolished in the 1960's. Today the spot where "Dark Annie" was found shortly before 6am on September the 8th is now a car park for a brewery company. The opposite side of the road is pretty much as it was in 1888 though. Often London graffiti gangs will come along and leave some kind of tribute to "Dark Annie" before the council remove it. If you walk to where the exact house would have been today, there's a large 29 on the pane of glass which marks where the front door of 29 Hanbury Street would be. If you walk right along down Hanbury Street you'll move onto Brick Lane and if you walk back up the other end, you'll be facing across the road to Spitalfields Market, next door to Christ Church, over the road from where the Ten Bells pub is (celebrity chef Jamie Oliver's great-great grandfather was the landlord in the 1880's) and where Dorset Street (13 Miller's Court) is where Mary Jane Kelly was killed. These are all within a stone's throw away from each other. This is what Paul Begg is referring to a little further on in this book when he says that Spitalfields is Jack the Ripper!!!

Hanbury Street does have other ties other than those relating to Jack the Ripper, incidentally Hanbury Street is the only Ripper murder location which still bares the same name that it did in 1888. Bud Flanagan was born at number 12 Hanbury Street. A blue plaque is up there today saying the same.

In April 1999 who can forget Neo-Naz militant David Copeland leaving a nail-bomb on Brick Lane. Copeland left the bomb on the corner of Hanbury Street/Brick Lane which would explode and tragically injure six people, destroying two vehicles in the process.

The third murder site which is Henriques Street (was Berner Street) has the eeriest feeling about it for me. I've been to all five murder sites several times but it's this one that really chills me. It is where Liz Stride, the first victim that night, was killed on September the 30th which was the night of the double event. At the top of the Street just before you come off Commercial Road there is graffiti saying in bold capitals, "ELISABETH STRIDE STREET 1843 – 1888". Thankfully, the local council street workers have seen it for what it is and have left it there as a mark of respect. As I was walking down what was Berner Street I realised that Batty Street is the street across and that was where the flamboyant Jack the Ripper suspect Dr Francis Tumblety was staying when its alleged he committed the murders.

There's now a children's playground on where Liz Stride was found at the old Dutfield's Yard. Stride had 'only' had her throat cut, which most Ripper experts acknowledge was probably down to Jack being disturbed by something or someone and because of that poor Catherine Eddowes got murdered less than an hour later. The sad thing is that if Jack hadn't of been disturbed, I don't think that Catherine Eddowes would have died that night. His insane thirst for cutting and ripping was denied with 'lucky Liz' and that is why he had to get it out of his system.

Many top police psychologists over the years have said what Jack did was never about extinguishing a life, it was the cutting, slashing, ripping and taking away the bits he did several times which really floated the killer's boat. When I was stood around looking at what was Dutfield's Yard, I realised just how close the other Ripper suspect Charles Cross (Lechmere) was to this particular scene. Not only did Charles Cross find the first of Jack's victims, Mary Nichols on Bucks Row, he also grew up within a stone's throw away from where Liz Stride was killed. Some argue that Cross was an innocent witness, other authors over the last few decades are convinced that he was the killer. I myself have to say that from a long line of fable contenders, the possibility of Charles Cross (Lechmere) being Jack has some real subsidence to it. Cross (Lechmere) is not only linked to the Whitechapel murders, but also to the Thames Torso Murders. Cross (Lechmere) grew up where Liz Stride was killed, and his mother lived very near at the time of the murders. There's also another theory that out of all the five Whitechapel killings in 1888, all were done on the route to Charles Cross' (Lechmere) work, and most were killed on his one night off in the week.

The fourth location is probably the most iconic and most visited by Ripper buffs over the years and that's Mitre Square. It's the only location where you can actually see something which is not put there by vandals or graffiti artists. There's a plaque up remembering Catherine Eddowes and telling a little bit of the square's history. Oddly very much like old Berner Street, the murder spot is on the corner of yet another children's playground. After researching on various ghostly forums and speaking to a Ripperologist, Mitre Square is apparently the most haunted out of the five murder scenes. There are stories on the grapevine that Catherine Eddowes' broken spirit can be seen on the anniversary of her death. It's also a hotbed for ghosthunters with their ghostbusting equipment trying to contact Catherine Eddowes.

On Halloween if you walk around Mitre Square it'll be extremely hectic. Over the years when I've been in London for various book projects, I've often just sat down in Mitre Square for a good hour and relayed everything in my mind, like how Catherine was seen by those three witnesses talking to the killer at the top of St James Passage, to how she was found only fifteen minutes later by the passing P.C Edward Watkins. As I sat there in the square alone my mind travelled back to the autumn of terror and I imagined just how noisy that little square would have been with police whistles, deafening copper's footsteps and shouts of, "THERE'S BEEN ANOTHER ONE" and the whole of the East End being in sheer panic. It was after that killing that Jack left his only clue which confirmed which way he had gone after the murder, there was also a rumour that they'd also found traces of blood at Aldgate pump, but nothing is factual on that.

The fifth and final murder scene was 13 Miller's Court which was just off Dorset Street which was just off Commercial Road. The reality now is you can't get anywhere near what was Mary Jane Kelly's bedsit as its now a plush office building so you can only look from a distance.

From my previous experience of walking around for twelve hours a day in London, if you want to walk into the murky streets of Jack the Ripper's 1888 then you only have to walk up Artillery Lane which is close to Liverpool Street Station. Artillery Lane was once known as 'Smock Alley' and it's easy to see why. Walking up that part of Spitalfields you can really see Jack the Ripper's London come back to life and if Jack could come back today and look around, that's the part from his old stomping ground that he'd recognise the most.

Another building which for me can be so surreal the more I stare at it is the old doss house, The Providence Row Refuge at 47 – 50 Crispin Street, Shoreditch. This place was also the location for The Crying Game film in 1992. Today it's lived in by young students but back in 1888 it was a workhouse which would house hundreds of men, women and children as long as you did a hard day's labour there. Still today in 2022 you can see above the entrances of who was allowed where, that to me really hits home just how unbearable living in Victorian times must have been for all who endured it. If you google Shoreditch/Spitalfields doss houses then you can see several pictures of men, women and children all queuing up for a bed for the night. Other parts of the East End where you can get the same effect as this is Gunthorpe Street which runs alongside the White Hart pub. Inspector Frederick Abberline's favourite suspect George Chapman (Seweryn Klosowski) once ran his barber shop from the pub's cellar which is still there today. The landlord of the White Hart pub told me recently that he often has Ripper buffs in his place on a weekly basis asking to go down to Chapman's old lair but for insurance reasons he can't let anyone down there. Just in case you were ever thinking of asking, I know this because I was also told no. Maybe Chapman wasn't Jack but overall, he was a killer. Chapman was convicted of murder and later hanged in 1903 in Wandsworth prison for poisoning three of his wives!

Many have suspected that there were more than five at the hands of Jack and that one of them was Martha Tabram (Turner). Tabram was killed only three weeks before the first publicly acknowledged killing of 'Polly' Nichols. Tabram was found at 5am in George's Yard which was just off Gunthorpe Street, so you see, everything is so close by i.e., Martha Tabram murder location to alleged Ripper's barber shop George Chapman. That's just one example so if you're interested like I am with the whole Whitechapel murder era then you can just turn up and google Whitechapel and the list of things to study and learn at the other end of a smartphone are endless.

"LONDON IS A BAD HABIT ONE HATES TO LOSE."

William Sansom

CHAPTER 8
A GHASTLY FIND IN MIDDLESBROUGH
by Richard Jones

On Friday, 13th December 1889, labourers unloading a barge of rubbish in Middlesbrough, discovered a woman's hand amongst the detritus.

Since the boat on which the hand was found had loaded its cargo of garbage in Millwall, London, some newspapers immediately linked it to the Whitechapel murders and questioned whether the hand may be from an unknown victim of Jack the Ripper.

The Daily Gazette for Middlesbrough immediately despatched a reporter to the scene to glean any information he could, and his account was published by the newspaper on Saturday, 16th 1889: "Whilst labourers there were working yesterday afternoon on board the Barque Picton Castle, one of the gangs discovered a woman's right hand perfect, save for the absence of two joints of the little finger.

Another labourer, by the name of McAulay, then stated that some time before he came across a bag containing something which emitted a fearful odour. Supposing that the bag contained dead cats, he threw it into the lighter, Flora, where it was then buried beneath a great quantity of ballast.

Information was at once given by McAulay to the Chief-Constable of Middlesbrough police, and, as the occurrence was not in his jurisdiction, the messenger was directed to go to the Durham side to report to Durham police.

Instructions were also given to institute a search in the lighter for the bag and its contents, which were then under a considerable amount of ballast.

It may be mentioned that this ballast was taken on board at Millwall, which is near enough to the part of the East of London where the recent series of fiendish atrocities which have horrified the whole country have been committed, to give reasonable colour to the surmise that the remains are those of another victim, till now undiscovered, of the monster who is widely known as "Jack the Ripper," thus concealed in shipping ballast, and brought to light at Middlesbrough.

The Picton Castle is a Barque. She arrived here on the 21st inst., and her ballast was put into her about a week before that time.

The ghastly discovery in the ballast on board the Barque Picton Castle in the Tees today continues to be the theme of much comment.

It was reported in one of the morning papers that the evil smelling bag referred to, which the stevedore's men threw into the lighter un-investigated, had been discovered, and that on being opened it was found to be filled with human remains in a very advanced state of decomposition. This report appears to have had its origin in some imaginative brain, since the bag has not been found, and has, in fact, scarcely been searched for as yet.

Our representative boarded the Picton castle this forenoon in quest of further information. But there is not much to add at present to what is given above.

Captain William Chalk, the master, had just gone ashore, but the mate, Mr Henry Thomas, was on board, and very ready to throw any light he could upon the mystery.

In reply to questions, he said that a police officer had just been on board and had taken away the hand.

"Have you found the bag yet that the men passed into the lighter?" asked our reporter.

"No," replied the mate;" they have not been looking for it yet." "But one of the papers says that the bag was found last night, and that it was full of human remains greatly decomposed?" "No, the bag is in the lighter under the ballast yet. But you had better see the stevedore; he can tell, you all about it."

Mr McAulay, the stevedore, here joined us, and was equally obliging in imparting all he knew of the matter. His statement as to the passing of the malodorous bag unopened into the lighter appears above. The bag, he said, was just an ordinary sack, with the month tied round.

"What was the condition of the bag?" enquired the reporter, "could the hand have fallen out of it?"

"That I could not say," replied Mr McAulay, "we did not examine the bag at the time." "Have not some other bones also been found?" "Yes, one of the men told me, after we found the hand, that he had turned some bones over, and one of them, he believed, was a human arm bone. But anyhow it was only just a dry bone and would have nothing to do with anything so recently dead as the hand."

"What was the hand like?" "It was small, a good deal swollen. We all took it to be a woman's hand; but the officer who came on board said he thought it was a man's hand. I think it was too small for that though. It was cut off clean at the wrist, and was in pretty good condition, but the two top joints of the little finger and the fingernails were gone."

"What kind of ballast was the hand found in?" "It was among ashes?" The mate, in answer to questions, here informed our reporter that the ballast was taken on board from lighters in the Millwall Dock. The loading of the ballast commenced on the 5th of November and was continued up to the 12th. The ballast consisted of two or three sorts – some dredged-up stuff from the river's bed, and some "shore rubbish."

"We left London," said he, "last Tuesday three weeks (26th November), and we arrived here the next Thursday in tow. The rubbish," he continued, "was shovelled out of the lighters into baskets and hoisted on board by the winch, as you see it being emptied now.

We were loading at night as well, and it is possible that the hand might have been shovelled in with the dirt at night and not noticed."

"Did you lie alongside the quay?" "Part of the time we lay alongside the quay, and part of the time we were out in the dock." "Then it is impossible the bag can have been put on board in the rubbish without the men noticing it? Don't you think it must have been smuggled on board by someone and put into the hold?"

"I can say, but I don't think anyone could have done so, as we were at work up to ten o'clock, and after that we had a watchman on duty." But watchmen sleep on duty occasionally, do they not?"

"Well, perhaps, they do. Anyhow, I have no theory at all as to how the bag or the hand got on board."

"Is it not possible that one of the labourers might have smuggled it on board?"

It is possible; some of them are bad enough to anything."

Our reporter then asked the stevedore whether any search had been made for the bag.

Mr McAulay said that his men had looked for it about half an hour, but then he had been obliged to take them off the search and put them upon their regular work.

"Have not the police put labourers on to search for it?"

"No; they wanted me to find men to do with it; but I have none to spare, and I cannot do their work."

"So, you have gone on since putting ballast into the lighter, and we are not likely to know for some time what is in the bag?"

"Yes; that is so."

"Have not the police done anything in the matter?"

"No; they have taken away the hand."

"It seems to me that I am about the only one who has been making enquiries into the matter?"

"Well, it is a fact that no one has asked so much about it as you have. We have had no one but you and the constable on board about it."

This was about the sum and substance of all that could be gathered on a vessel. (It should be stated that in all probability the dates given on leaving London are a week too recent, judging by the time that the loading of ballast was completed)

Our reporter then went in quest of the police, who have the matter in hand.

Nearby there was only a works policeman, who seemed to have had no material connection with the case, and the next nearest officer was a constable at Haverton Hill. He was out in connection with the case and could not be found at that salubrious village.

Our reporter, however, discovered him later, with the ghastly remnant of humanity swinging innocently on a string from his hand in a brown paper parcel.

After the manner of his August calling the officer was reticent and disposed to make as little as possible of the matter.

As to the question of whether the hand was that of a man or woman, he declined to commit himself to a reporter, observing that it was a question for a medical man. He thought the hand must have been dead eight or nine weeks and explained that it would decompose much more slowly than other parts of the body, all the blood being out of it.

The officer replied, "We cannot search for it. It is under tons of ballast, and the lighter is full. There is nowhere to empty the ballast to look for it. We shall not be able to see what is in the bag until the lighter is discharged in the usual way, which will be about the middle of next week. Sergeant Cameron, of Stockton has the case in hand, and your representative at Stockton will know all about it, as soon as there is anything to know."

In reply to further questions the officer remarked that he thought that there was nothing in it, and that the bag would probably be found to contain dead dogs or cats. If that was so, there was only the hand to go upon, and there was no knowing where the hand has come from; the ballast was often passed from one ship to another.

As to whether the hand was a man's or a woman's, no medical man had seen it up to the time of the interview with the Haverton Hill constable.

The thumb, in removing the packing in paper parcel, has dropped off the hand. It is undoubtedly a small hand, and though one police officer has opined it to be that of a man, all the crew of the vessel and the stevedores' men and one or two others who have seen it are unanimous in believing it to be that of a woman.

The case thus stands exactly where it did when the hand was first discovered, and in all probability, we shall know nothing further until the lighter is emptied, in the usual course, about the middle of next week."

The Daily Gazette for Middlesbrough published an update on the case in its edition of Monday 16th December 1889:

"On Saturday evening, the hand which was found on Friday in the ballast on board the Swansea Barque Picton Castle from Millwall, which was discharging in the Tees, was removed to Stockton and examined by Dr. Foss.

This gentleman expressed the opinion that it was the right hand of a full-grown female; it was in an advanced stage of decomposition. The hand had been separated from the wrist, Dr. Foss believes, after death, and that gentleman is also of the opinion that the hand has been for some months either in water or in a very damp place.

This has led to a hypothesis on the part of the police that the hand has been dredged up in the soil from the bed of the Thames, or dug up from the foreshore, and is probably that of some drowned person.

The clean severance from the wrist, however, seems to call for some further explanation.

Although the Haverton Hill constable informed our representative on Saturday morning that no search could be made for the bag of suspected human remains which was shot into the lighter Flora, un-investigated, and covered with ballast before the hand was found, until the lighter was discharged in the usual course, some constables went on board on Saturday night and made a search for the bag, which, however, they were unable to find.

It was first arranged that the lighter Flora should be discharged at Connal's wharf, but as it was found that she would not be able to take a turn there until Wednesday Mr Henderson, the proprietor, decided to discharge her ballast out at the sea today.

When our reporter boarded the Picton Castle between eleven and twelve this morning the lighter was still alongside, and the ballast was still being unloaded.

The mate stated that he was expecting that the lighter would be towed off to be emptied directly.

Therefore, up to the present the case has only been advanced by the medical opinion of Dr. Foss. who confirms the general opinion as to the hand being that of a woman; but those opinions as to the length of time that the hand has been dead, and as to its probable long immersion, rather militates against the theory of another recent "Thames Mystery" or "Jack the Ripper" horror.

In discharging the lighter a careful look-out for the bag will be kept, and when found it will be handed over to the police to investigate."

Then, on Wednesday 18th December 1889, the Gazette revealed that the missing sack had been found, albeit its contents proved to be something of an anti-climax:

"Owing to the high wind which prevailed on Monday Mr Henderson's lighter Flora was not discharged at sea, as had been intended.

Yesterday the wind has still further freshened, and the lighter was taken to Connal's Wharf to be discharged.

The work of unloading was commenced shortly after one o'clock, and-a-half hours without anything being seen of the bag which had been tipped into the boat with the ballast from the Picton Castle.

The bottom was almost cleared when, in the one corner where the soil had not been removed, the bag was found.

It was, as Mr McAulay, the stevedore, described, a common sack tied round the mouth with some string.

It was at once hauled up to the wharf and opened in the presence of Superintendent Bell, from Stockton, who had been watching the proceedings throughout, and of Detective Superintendent Thorpe, and a number of Press representatives.

On being opened the long-sought-for bag was found to contain earth of guano, full of fibrous matter, and emitting no particular odour. Consequently, the fearful smell which the stevedore's men described appears to have been conjured up by a memory of a too flexible character.

Therefore, the supposed tragedy rests entirely upon the right hand of a woman which was found in the ballast on Friday afternoon.

The hand will probably be buried now, and its presence in ballast and who has been its owner will probably forever remain a mystery."

"MURDER IS AS GOOD A SUBJECT AS ANY OTHER."

Walter Sickert, Artist & Ripper Suspect

CHAPTER 9
COME ON WEST HAM

As someone growing up in the Northeast, my view is that West Ham, along with Newcastle United fans, are the best fans in English football. The one thing the proper Cockney is passionate about apart from the old fight game is football. Most of the East Enders are Happy Hammers. Although they've never really won anything in my lifetime, the West Ham fans are there for their team through wind, rain and snow. Often West Ham are described as, 'everybody's second team' and I very much get it. I mean, how could you not like West Ham United compared to the likes of Manchester United, Chelsea and Leeds United. People are maybe unaware that all the stars such as Geoff Hurst, Sir Bobby Moore (the darling of the East End), Nigel Spink, Ray Houghton, Tony Cottee, Paul Ince, John Terry, Rio Ferdinand, Frank Lampard, Michael Carrick, Joe Cole, Kieron Richardson, Jermain Defoe, and Glen Johnson all started with West Ham. If you put all of them together in one team and West Ham didn't sell them on for obvious reasons, they could have won the bloody Champions League.

I was lucky enough to speak with former West Ham striker Frank McAvennie recently for another book on Celtic icon Alan Thompson. When I was growing up, because of my Scottish parentage and living in Glasgow for a time in my life, I've always been Celtic mad. Frank McAvennie is a God up in Glasgow with the green & white half of the city for what he achieved in Celtic's century season of 1987/88. Today as a 42-year-old I have signed memorabilia of Macca up in my house, but back as an 8-year-old boy I had the Celtic kit, and I was Frank McAvennie when it came to kicking a ball around the playground. I used to grow the blonde mullet like Frank because I wanted to be him. Well because of what Frank did with West Ham alongside Tony Cottee in the 1980's, Frank McAvennie is bigger in the East End of London than Glasgow and that's saying something because I know how much Macca is adored by the masses of Celtic support.

You only have to look at the stars that support them such as boxer Kevin Mitchell, the band Cockney Rejects, Stepney hardman Roy Shaw, Russell Brand, Trevor Brooking, Frank Bruno, Sir Alfred Hitchcock, James Corden, Noel Edmonds, Danny Dyer, Ray Winstone, Ricky Grover, Nick Berry, Ross Kemp, Lennox Lewis, Helen Mirren, Kiera Knightly, Pixie Lott, Billy Murray, Glen Murphy to see how fanatical there are about their team. Even people such as Katie Perry, Matt Damon, Barack Obama, Gennady Golovkin and Queen Elizabeth have spoken of their love of West Ham United. The reason this book has the name that it has is because of another West Ham loving celebrity, but you wouldn't believe it and that's Morrissey. The 80's icon is obsessed with the whole East End thing and that's the reason he walked around with West Ham Boys Club jumpers on in his days with The Smiths. He's also been pictured on Whitechapel Road outside of the old Grave Maurice for album covers and has written songs about Jack the Ripper, Charlie Richardson and Ronnie & Reggie Kray. Morrissey is even said to have sent both twins wreaths on the day of their funerals.

The main rivalry in London in my opinion isn't Arsenal v Tottenham Hotspur like you'd imagine, its Millwall v West Ham United, certainly if you're going for bad blood between the pair. The fixture is always pretty nasty, and it's boiled over into trouble on the terraces many times over the decades. The rivalry between the two is one of the longest-standing and bitter in the game. I suppose the reason for the rivalry would come from when both teams started off, then known as Millwall Athletic and Thames Ironworks they both came from the East End of London and only three miles apart. The first time they clashed was in the 1899/1900 season in the F.A Cup. The fixture was known as the Dockers derby, as both sets of supporters were predominately dockers at shipyards on either side of the river Thames. In 1904 Ham moved to the Boleyn Ground which was then Essex until a London boundary changed in 1965. In 1910 Millwall moved over to South London and that's when it was no longer an 'East End fixture'. Today both teams are four miles apart and it hasn't got any more peaceful in the 99 times they've met each other. Millwall have won 38, West Ham 34 with 27 ending in a share of the points.

Whitechapel very much graced England with the greatest fullback football has ever seen in Ashley Cole who started off with Arsenal, then went on to represent his country 107 times, not to mention marry the stunning Cheryl Tweedy from Girls Aloud. The boy from the East End, who went to school in Bow, is a huge success story and an inspiration to many of the young kids in Whitechapel.

Overall, I don't know much about West Ham because I grew up in Middlesbrough but from an outsiders view the West Ham fans, alongside the Geordies, are the most passionate in English football. Players such as Paul Ince and Dimitri Payet will forever be known as Judas' to the supporters, whilst others such as Paolo Di Canio, Mr West Ham himself Mark Noble and Carlton Cole will never have to buy a pint in the West Ham pubs for the rest of their lives.

As the West Ham fans say, come on you Irons and I'm forever blowing bubbles, pretty bubbles in the air which is usually blaring out by 'Stinky Turner' from The Cockney Rejects, I can only imagine what the old Upton Park would have been like when it was rocking with 35,000 East Enders. If it was anything like when local fighter Kevin Mitchell fought the Aussie Michael Katsidis in the summer of 2010 it must have been euphoric because that was unbelieve viewing, if you forget about the boy from the East End getting bashed that is. I myself had dinner with Dagenham's Mitchell in 2017 around Spitalfields Market and was blown away at just how Cockney he was. To us Northerners it is really like listening to a foreign language at times.

Overall, West Ham will always be my second team just like everyone else's. I bet you're reading this now and thinking, well actually I've never minded West Ham United! The passion the proper Cockney has for the beautiful game is second to none. Maybe one day some rich billionaire will come and buy West Ham United like the owners of Newcastle Utd. I can't think of any English set of fans like the East Enders who deserve it more.

"Someone said I wasn't a proper Cockney the other day by calling me a 'mockney', so I threw him down the apples & oranges."

Chas 'Diamond' Geezer

CHAPTER 10
CHRIS ROSS - THE EASTEND POET

One guy I came across during the research for this book was the East End Poet, Chris Ross. After watching his YouTube channel and other social media pages I knew I had to speak with him. It was like Chris had just walked off the set of Oliver Twist and for me he epitomises exactly what this book is about. Chris just ticked every box in the auld Cockney department, so I knew I just had to chat with him for this book. I was honoured that Chris spared me a little time early one Friday morning in February 2022 before he went down Kelly's on Roman Road for his usual Cockney grub pie & mash.

Chris said: –

I was born in 1954 in Mile End Hospital, East London. For the first few years of my life, I was brought up just behind Mile End Station on a street that's not there anymore, then when I was around 14 my family moved over to Roman Road and we settled there for good. The Roman Road Market and everything that surrounds it is basically who I am.

I was essentially brought up through the 1960's and London's changed hugely since those days. Change is a very funny thing. I mean, I'm sure if you asked my old mum in the 1960's what the area is like now compared to when she grew up, she'd think exactly the same as I do. Mum was born in 1927 and I've only just lost her, but she lived in London through the war.

When I look back to the 1960's in London everything seemed to burst into colour from the black & white we'd lived in before. of course, everything in 2022 is in colour. Everything in life changes and I have to laugh at my fellow East Enders going on saying, 'oh

London isn't what it was', guess what, neither are you! It's the circle of life and of course London is a very different place to even the decade previously. Everything and everyone evolve! I often hear that cliché of, 'oh we used to know everyone down our street back in the day' and yes that's all very true. I mean I've lived where I am now in Beckton for 35 years and I couldn't tell you who lives down the end of my road. If you offered me £1000 to name the next street from me, I couldn't tell you, but back growing up in the East End I knew the whole map of the entire area. Today I class it as just where I live, but back then it was who I was and what I was about. The East End is who Chris Ross is. Back during the 60's I knew everyone in the whole manor.

Today I live in the East of London but it's not the East End. The East End is a different animal altogether. Just because you've got an East London postcode that doesn't mean you're a real East Ender. The proper East End for me is Stepney, Mile End, Bethnal Green, Whitechapel, Poplar and Bow. Anything outside of that and it's not the East End, its East London.

Today when I walk back along Roman Road where I used to live, I will see the odd folk I know, but it's not like years ago when I knew every single person about and that's how the East End has changed so much because it's not like that anymore.

When I go back to the real East End, although the street I was brought up in has gone, there's still a lot there to see if I look hard enough when I drive around. As kids for us in the East End the streets were our playground. Things like cemeteries were our play areas and when I go back there and close my eyes, it's like walking into my childhood. When the local council pulled down my old street, they did so on the promise that it would be replaced by a 'street in the sky'! They said instead of being next door to each other we'd be on top of each other but in fact we never got streets in the sky. What we did get was broken lifts and shattered glass which just looked an absolute eyesore. It was never going to be the same and that's what's happened to a lot of the East End community. I'm aware that the thing about change is that it's inevitable, the circle of life in society has to happen. For instance, the house I grew up in had an outside toilet and we bathed in an old tin bath which we used to drag inside to put in front of the fire, can you imagine doing that in this day and age? That's my point and why change has to happen in life I'm afraid!

By the time I'd left school the Kray Twins were in prison, although they were still spoken of in the East End, but they were long gone. What has happened when I've told people on holidays that I'm from the East End of London is usually what comes next is, "oh so did you know Ronnie & Reggie Kray?" That has happened so many times over the decades, and I've got to be honest with you, I can't help but think, 'oh would you just give me a bloody break will you'?! The reality of it all was that they were just a couple of thugs and that was it. Listen my old mum knew them and my dad knew them quite well. I mean, back then, the East End was a small place. Today you wouldn't know someone just because they lived in the East End but back then through the 60's you knew everyone.

The Jack the Ripper thing, which I know this book is mainly about, we all love a 'who done it/mystery' don't we, well this was the ultimate of that kind. I'm sure they'll go on and on with making films about the murders of Whitechapel because it's so historic, not to mention it captures that Victorian age. At that time in London, it was only good if you had a few quid and if you never, well it was hell on earth quite simply! My ancestors lived in real rural poverty which this country will never see again. In all of these fancy movies on Jack they neglect that side of real life and its more about the fancy toff who went around Whitechapel cutting people up. Another thing about this Jack the Ripper myth, if somebody asked, 'so what does Jack the Ripper look like?' Then the answer would be dressed in black, top hat, cape, carries a swagger stick in one hand, with a Gladstone bag in the other for all his knives. The reason that we have this image is because that's what the media have told us he looked like for the past 134 years. The bottom line of it, if I had to put my life on it, was that Jack the Ripper looked like a right dirtbag who's only skill was killing people! The media have always glorified Jack's invented look haven't they?

In most gangster films there has to be a villain in there from the East End, such as in the Guy Ritchie films. There are people out there that want to define the East End with this type of thing, and it isn't who we really are! Look I can't get away from the fact that there's always been a bit of villainy/skulduggery going on but not what the books and film portray.

I once wrote a song and one of the lyrics in it was, 'we always had a spirit of free enterprise' and you can take that in any way you want it to mean. People in the East End have grown up in scenarios where these goods could be offered to them for a third of the price and so of course they wouldn't ask questions. It was just seen as the norm in the East End. I would often ask my old mum where she got things from and she would say, "oh it come along" (laughs) which means, someone flogged her it for a quick buck. That was very much your typical East End saying, "it come along" like it just walked into someone's house on its own.

I was told years ago that if you write about what you know then it's usually more interesting. That's why most of what I write about in my poems or the songs I sing are about West Ham

United. I've been asked in the past why I don't ever write anything about Tottenham Hotspur and the answer is simple, I'm not a Spurs fan and I know nothing about them. Although I did write a song called, 'I'm Not a Tottenham Supporter' (laughs). I can't write about what I don't know but what I do know about is all of the stuff such as the East End, Cockney rhyming slang, pie & mash, jellied eels, West Ham, Chas & Dave etc... If I wanted to write about anything else, I'd have to sit there for hours on end researching the internet. What I actually write about doesn't take any effort whatsoever because it's what I'm all about and what I do. Everything in my field comes naturally and its honest which I can relate to. I may write about other things but it's things I know like my wife, kids and grandchildren. With me writing poems and songs about all what I do, it allows me to get out what I'm feeling and that's extremely therapeutic. All the stuff I bleed out helps me emotionally and I'm happy for the day. I do enjoy pulling off a few covers of good auld Cockney rock Chas & Dave. If other people enjoy my work at the same time, then that's even better. This morning before you interviewed me, I recorded myself reciting a poem called, 'I fancy pie & mash today' and that's something which comes from a true event because I'll be going with the guvnor (wife) after I finish speaking to you for this book. I uploaded my poem of me belting out, 'I fancy pie & mash today' and put it on Twitter, Facebook and YouTube and that's my contribution for this morning and it keeps me happy until I do the next one.

On the subject of Cockney rhyming slang that is something that changes with the times in London also. Quite recently I was in the East End, and I overheard someone talking about their 'Britney Spears' which obviously means 'beers'. As I heard that I thought, she's only a young kid isn't she so that just goes to show you how this unique slang moves with the times. To be honest I don't know if people in the East End use it as much as people who aren't from the area think. Of course, you've got your standard ones such as 'apples & pears' (stairs) which everyone knows but it's not widely spoken as such on a daily basis anymore and to be honest I'm not sure it ever was. It's always been there in the background but if anyone strings more than one word of slang in a conversation then you might as well turn into Danny Dyer! Nobody really talks like him really! It's just badly exaggerated for his movies and documentaries.

Sports have always been very big for the boys in our manor, things such as football and boxing. The fight game in particular is a big thing and I'm going to tell you the reason why. When you go back to the early days and well before I was born, life was bloody hard growing up in the old East End and boys looked for an escape and pugilism brought exactly that! Regarding the football, nine times out of ten you'd support your local side which was usually West Ham United. When I first started following The Hammers it was 1964 and, in that year, they won the F.A Cup. I'll never forget as a 9-year-old boy West Ham coming down the Mile End Road on an open top bus holding the trophy. Looking at the colours of claret & blue that day with Sir Bobby Moore at the front of the bus holding the cup up to show all of us fans, it was magical. The year after West Ham won the European Cup Winners Cup and then the year after in 1966, England won the World Cup and Sir Bobby lifted that as well. To me, as just a young boy, in my mind I thought West Ham United were the greatest team in the whole wide world. The unfortunate thing for me then is I grew up and learnt what being a West Ham supporter is all about which is that it's not all sunshine and rainbows let me tell you.

My first heroes growing up and going to Upton Park were Sir Bobby Moore, Geoff Hurst and Martin Peters. I used to love watching Harry Redknapp and Frank Lampard Snr. I'd get on the train at Mile End and go up to Upton Park and all the old geezers would look after you and say, "go on boy down the front you go" and you were looked after. Often, I would be standing like three feet away from Harry Redknapp taking a corner, being of such a young age it was magical to be in such close proximity to your hero's. Us West Ham fans will always appreciate our heroes if they play for the shirt. Your names like Frank McAvennie, Paolo Di Canios and even Dimitri Payet, before he turned Judas on our club. God he was loved before he turned sham and the way he left. We've also had some cracking oldies towards the end of their careers such as Teddy Sheringham and Nigel Winterburn who've done a job for us. I'm actually old enough to remember the great Jimmy Greaves coming to West Ham. We sold Martin Peters to Spurs and part of the deal was Greavesy come to us. I remember Jimmy as a great player, he was the best and was unlucky to just miss out of playing in the World Cup Final for England in 1966 through injury. Alf Ramsey, the gaffer of the team, knew he couldn't have lasted 90 minutes and Geoff Hurst got the nod so he missed out and the rest is history as they say, but as a player he was out of this world as a goal scorer. To just see him in a West Ham shirt even at the end of his career was still a great sight as he was the greatest striker England has ever seen in my opinion.

Today with all the crap going on over Ukraine I worry about the future of the world, let alone along Roman Road. The future is bright for the East End and I'm glad it's not like it used to be back in the day when everyone struggled. When I hear people having a whinge about missing the old days I think, I tell you what you miss about the old days, you miss your youth! Things such as your mum cooking your dinner and your dad paying your rent! Being young and doing exactly what we wanted to do without having any responsibilities. I mean, what's to miss about going to the outside toilet in the middle of the night? Having a bath in front of the fire? Oh, please do me a favour! The future is as bright as what you want to make it really! My fellow East Enders always look on the bright side of life because there's always a bright side. If people want to be happy in life, then they must accept change! Not necessarily embrace it, but you have to accept it to increase one's happiness. Change in life is going to happen anyway so there's no point rallying against it. For instance, as I'm talking to you for this book there's a load of stuff going on over in Russia. A prime example of the point I'm trying to make is, what can I do about Wladimir Putin? The answer is absolutely nothing at all so all I can do is go out for pie & mash today and roll with the punches that life throws at me! We all need to look for the fun in life because we're not here long enough to bother. I lost my mum only a couple of weeks ago and that really kind of put things into perspective, and although she was 94 it made me think, well that could be me next!

If anyone would like to follow Chris' work, you can do on –

FACEBOOK – Chris Ross, The East End Poet

TWITTER - @TheEastEndPoet

INSTAGRAM – theeastendpoet

YOUTUBE – http://www.youtube.com/user/MyChrisRoss

"I LONG TO GO THROUGH THE CROWDED STREETS OF YOUR MIGHTY LONDON, TO BE IN THE MIDST OF THE WHIRL AND RUSH OF HUMANITY, TO SHARE ITS LIFE, ITS CHANGE, ITS DEATH, AND ALL THAT MAKES IT WHAT IT IS."

Bram Stoker, Dracula.

CHAPTER 11
Richard Jones
NO.1 RIPPER EXPERT IN THE WORLD
(In my opinion)

I was brought up in Stoke on Trent so that makes me a Potter. I stayed in Stoke until I was around 11 before I went to a seminary to learn to become a priest. I stayed there until I was 15. I was asked to leave because I said I didn't believe in God anymore, I mean, if you're going to choose the fatherhood then not believing in the powers of above kind of limit your potential. I went back to Stoke for a short time, back to my parents until I was around 18, that's when I left Stoke for the bright lights of London. I decided to find my fortune in the capital, and I got a job as a civil servant.

I came to London around Halloween time in 1977 not knowing a single soul. At this time all the strikes were happening so London was pretty bleak. I managed to secure some digs in Acton, and I'll never forget my journey through London in darkness and seeing all the rubbish piled up along the streets. It was very different to how I'd been living back home in Stoke on Trent. At that time, I played the guitar, wrote songs and wrote bits of poetry, not to mention thought of myself as a bit of a potential popstar.

When I was in my second accommodation, which was basically a hotel, it was a place where people first go when they go to find their fortunes in London and are just starting out. After a while of being in there, I found the Troubadour Club where Paul Simon and Bob Dylan were discovered in London. I went down there one Monday night in hope that I too would be discovered as I played my guitar as a punk/folk singer. I did that for a while as I was finding my feet in the city.

After having several little jobs in offices as being a kind of 'tea boy' I saw a job advert in the London paper to be a postman. I applied for the vacancy and I got the job. My route on the job was around King Edward building near St Paul's Cathedral. That's really when I first started walking around this truly amazing city and starting to see all its historic magical history. After walking around in my new post, I realised that many of the street names I was familiar with because of my love for Charles Dickens. I then started mapping things out in my head when I was delivering letters, I was also discovering Charles Dickens walks in the city of London. To be honest I first started doing this for my own entertainment.

One day when I was telling a fellow postman about who, when and where Charles Dickens was, he told me that he had some friends coming over from America, and would I mind taking them on a tour around these places and explaining the history to them. I did end up taking this group around talking all about arguably Great Britain's most famous writer and I loved it. After the brilliant feedback I received from the Americans they suggested I do it professionally. After a little bit of thinking I thought ok I'll give it a go, so I put an advert in London Time Out one Sunday evening in 1982 for a ghost walk from Bank Station and 18 people turned up. Over a time, and to cut a long story short, I quit working for Royal Mail and fully focused on my walking tours across London. Looking back, I got too carried away with it at first because I found there's a big difference in doing something like that as a hobby, then trying to make a living out of it fulltime. When I got membership of the London tourist board that gave me access to promote accordingly. I found I was a natural with the ghost, legal London and Charles Dickens walks.

At that point I still hadn't met Jack the Ripper, but it was inevitable because it was approaching the centenary year, which was a big thing among Ripper buffs. When I began doing the Jack the Ripper stuff I was living in Hackney. Yes, I'd heard about Jack at that time, but I knew virtually nothing about it, although most East Enders would always talk about Jack. I'll never forget being in a pub just off the back of Whitechapel Road around the early 1980's and found that there were two subjects the locals were always talking about, and they were the Krays and Jack the Ripper! At this point Ronnie & Reggie Kray had been in prison for 15 years and some phantom figure known as Jack who nobody even knew the identity of had been gone 100 years. It was unbelievable how all the old timers who knew Ronnie & Reggie from the good old days would talk about them like they still had their liberty.

When I put together the walk on Jack, I would start at Tower Hill Station and make a halfway stop at the Frying Pan pub on Brick Lane, it wasn't an Indian restaurant like it is now it was a pub, and it was run by an ex-boxer who knew the twins. I can still see him in my mind as he used to wear the same cardigan and although grumpy, it was his act to be grumpy! He was actually a really nice guy as he stood behind the bar with his boxers features from yesteryears ring battles. From there my tour would go on down Whitechapel Road and I'd finish in Ronnie Kray's favourite pub, The Grave Maurice. When I used to sit among the old faces of the East End the stories used to be fantastic. Everyone grew up in the area and particularly in the Grave Maurice, every old guy I met in there said he used to work for the Krays. Whether it was true or not I don't know, however it was almost always the topic of conversation in there. Also, all the old senior citizens would tell anyone who'd listen things like, 'oh back in the day when the twins were about you could walk our manor and not worry' or things like, 'you could leave your front door open' etc... Some of the old women would say things like, my old grandma met Jack the Ripper one night and he said to her, 'I can see you're a good girl so I'm going to let you live'. Old tales like that were often rife among the old dears of the East End.

As I first got familiar with the area of Whitechapel, I did feel a bit uneasy because of all the horror stories that came with it, but when I started doing the Jack the Ripper tours on the manor you just become part of the furniture. I became just like everyone else in the area i.e., shopkeepers, takeaway owners or landlords who were making a living. As I got to really know the area inside out, I thought, hang on a minute, it's not really that scary after all! The more I got to know every inch of Whitechapel the more it felt like home. Today in 2022 I still wander the area morning, noon and night and I never feel uneasy in any part of it. Whitechapel is only scary to those who don't know it or have just heard all about its dreaded history. Yes, the place has its fair share of shady characters, but it also has had its Lionel Bart's (produced the music and lyrics to Oliver Twist) the British writer or Lew Grade the British media proprietor although they rarely get mentioned enough because of the dark side of the area.

The area of Whitechapel as a whole is still new to me, I still have that feeling that I'm on holiday when I walk the streets. For instance, if I ever feel a bit depressed, I'll just say to the wife, I'm off for a walk around Whitechapel because it's my favourite part of the city. Whitechapel is the place of London with the most variety. If ever I've got a problem and feeling low, I find a walk around the place fixes that. If I'm say in a church in Whitechapel on a downer I think, someone was in here like 500 years ago feeling like I am now, and now their long since gone. Then I think someone else will be standing here in another 500 years from now with the same emotions and that puts it into perspective.

Whitechapel as a whole has seen hardship and poverty like no other place in the UK, and it faced it head on. Whitechapel hasn't run away from its problems. The area has at times had the eyes of the world on it for all the wrong reasons and it doesn't hide. People I think can learn a lot from good old Whitechapel, I know I certainly have.

During the horrendous times of hardship, although other areas such as Southwark and Notting Dale maybe had even worse conditions than Whitechapel in the late 19th century, but of course Whitechapel was the one that everybody focused on because of the murders. This is the reason why Jack the Ripper had the impact he did in the years after the killings because it could have only gotten better after the monstrosities of 1888. For instance, if Jack had slaughtered them women in a different area of London, I don't think he would have created the impact he did. Of course, in 1888 the term 'East Enders' had only just come about, and it gave out this image of an area which was beyond the border.

If you read what the social commentators of Whitechapel had to say around about this time, then they talk about it like the place was becoming a third world country. The people around are described as 'savages' or as Jack London described them as, 'people of the abysses and its missionaries are going into Whitechapel.' The people of Whitechapel turned into everything that people should be afraid of in the 19th century. With many afraid of the area and everyone in it, it then built up this mysticism, for instance all of the Americans that were coming over during this time always did a tour of Whitechapel. The place was famous throughout the world for its degradation and depravity. Folk were intrigued to know, 'is it really as bad as people say'? The scary thing was, it really was as bad as the horror stories, although the whole area wasn't like that! There were certain parts of Whitechapel which were even as plush as parts of the fancy West End. The worst part of Whitechapel in the Jack the Ripper generation was Flower & Dean Street, it was as bad as anything could ever get during that time.

I myself have written so many books on Jack the Ripper as well as doing the tours. I've shown a few old famous faces around, such as the American comedian Joan Rivers and a few more I can't name out of confidentiality. Although many of the real East Enders don't like to talk about it, there's no denying that Jack the Ripper has brought a lot of people trade and helped the economy since the autumn of terror.

Regardless of your emotions surrounding the whole case, it's something most people on this planet have heard about and I mean that across the world over. Even if most aren't clued up on the story, they're still aware of this caped phantom that supposedly carried a gladstone bag and killed a few women. Even if they only know of his trademark name most people are aware that once upon a time there was this hideous monster in darkened Victorian England.

People today still shout out and refer to me as the 'Jack the Ripper guy' which I find comical. If you saw a painter & decorator walking down the street nobody would shout his trade at him, would they?! One very funny old tale with me and Jack the Ripper, I just must tell you for this book. When my eldest son Thomas was 7, I went to pick him up from school and his teacher called me to one side. I thought, 'oh no what's he done now' but the teacher just laughed and said she must tell me what happened in class that day. She went on to tell me her and all the children had had this 'what does my dad do' day. Many of the children were standing up saying things like, 'my dad is an accountant, banker or shopkeeper etc... She told me that my Thomas stood up in front of the whole class as proud as punch and announced, "my dad's Jack the Ripper" (laughs). It's not as ludicrous a statement really because Jack the Ripper bought my house!

Throughout 40 years of doing the Jack the Ripper tours the only problem I've had in Whitechapel is young kids firing water pistols at me, or maybe the odd egg or two on mischief night. Even though I do what I do for a living, and I don't live in Whitechapel I like the area. If I'm not at work I will still go into Whitechapel in the pubs in my own time. There used to be this wonderful little pub on Brick Lane which isn't there anymore called The Alma. The Alma was the type of place which had all the old East End villains/faces usually in it. The landlord was Steve Kane who'd been a bit of an actor and knew all the old gangsters from the Kray brother's era. Steve was close with and had done a bit of acting with Dennis Waterman, who only recently sadly passed away, so they filmed a few episodes of Minder in the pub. There would always be a Rolls Royce parked outside of the bar. Even though they were all old men in there, you still wouldn't have wanted to cross any of these figures from London's underworld. When I used to talk to all of these ex-bank robbers, bareknuckle fighters or gangland figures they were always really lovely to me, but I did used to hear the odd story about what these folk were linked with, and it made me glad I was just a nobody in that aspect.

Ironically talking about The Alma and Jack the Ripper, the owners did the back room out and made it into a museum of Jack the Ripper and it was like that for a number of years. The original sign for the Jack the Ripper pub (which was the Ten Bells in Spitalfields) was also in there with all the old news articles from 1888. Sadly, Steve Kane, I believe, got into cocaine and died early from a heart-attack.

Today in 2022 you see all types of merchandise regarding the murders which I find really tasteless. I have no problem with people doing books or documentaries because that's educational, but the other things mentioned in one of the chapters further back in the book is just not for me. One story in the centenary year of 1988 I heard was that the Ten Bells, which at the time was called The Jack the Ripper, started dying all the beer red to look like pints of blood. Other drinks were called the 'Ripper tipple'. Of course, it wasn't long before some incredibly angry people started campaigning outside of the pub with signs protesting and encouraging people not to go into the premises.

When I started doing the tours back in the early 80's the Ten Bells is nothing like it is today. Back then the landlord Ernie really used to hit all that merchandise stuff in the bar hard. The pub was always selling t-shirts, posters, mugs etc...

Back then Spitalfields Market was still just a fruit market and lots of prostitutes literally hung around the doors. Many of the truck drivers dropping off at the market would provide a constant economy for the working ladies. Many of the working girls through the 1980's would come into the Ten Bells to clean up after being with a client just like they did 100 years before. The landlord Ernie knew of the girls and to be honest they were all a great laugh, respectful and it didn't put the punters off their gin. Some of the girls were even getting clients saying, 'I wanna go do it with a whore on a Jack the Ripper murder location' because that was their kink. If ever me or Martin Fido (God rest him) would walk past they'd shout at us, "same again tonight darling", with a great sense of humour. Today all of that is long gone and you'd have to travel to places like Hackney to see that type of thing. There used to be two types of working girls, with one it was their profession and they would have a laugh with you, then there were the addicts who kept themselves to themselves after doing what they needed to do. I would always feel really sorry for both but more so the drug addicts because they weren't doing it out of choice like the others were. The red-light district was always outside of Christ Church until the police chased them all away to Hackney Green. Around 1993 the area was totally cleaned up of kerb crawlers by the authorities. I do love that little corner on Commercial Road of the Ten Bells, Christ Church and Spitalfields Market.

If I had to tell you readers my opinion on who Jack was then in all honesty, I wouldn't even know where to begin. It must have been the guy who everyone thought was a little bit strange but harmless, everyone avoided him, and he wasn't even noticed by the press reporters, but every now and then the voices in his head got too much and he had to go and act on them. Whoever he was he was obviously a deranged narcissist and I very much doubt he thought he would be making his mark in the history books 134 years on. I think his only thoughts were about killing those poor women that he murdered.

I would have to say that Gunthorpe Street just off Whitechapel Road is the spot from the whole area that I feel like I'm in Jack's era the most. Walking past the White Hart pub along up to where George's Yard, where Martha Tabram was killed, is almost like slipping into a portal of Whitechapel 1888.

Although I've lived in London now more than I've lived anywhere else, my pottery accent does come back now and again, however I definitely consider myself as some sort of adopted East Ender. Both my sons are well and truly Londoners, and my wife was just South of Kent, so I'm outnumbered with Cockney accents in our home. We're in East London and have the postcode to prove it. I always like to tell people I live three streets away from Alan Sugar, which I do, but it's the North Circular Road, M25 and the M11 (laughs).

Many real East Enders today live outside of the East End. These days you can hear more proper Cockney accents in Southend than you do in the East End. For as long as I'm alive I don't think I'll ever not say to the wife, 'right love I feel a bit down so I'm off for a walk around Whitechapel to cheer myself up'. Even today 40 years later I still make discoveries in the East End. For instance, I've just discovered St Dunstan's Church in Stepney which I'd never even noticed before. It's so bizarre because as I was walking down Mile End Road, I saw this church steeple, so I went to have a look. I've never noticed this amazing building and it was right in the spiritual heart of the East End of London. It's things like that which can happen all the time which is fantastic. Even today the East End is still showing me all of these magical places which are steeped in history. So often I'll walk around the city and although I've walked past there hundreds of times, I've never quite noticed a certain building and London does this to me often. It's a bit like when you look in the mirror and see a freckle or some blemish that you've never noticed on your neck before, but it's always been your body!

If you want to get in touch with Richard, you can on the following

Twitter - @RipperTours

Instagram – The Jack the Ripper Tour

Facebook – Jack the Ripper Tours

YouTube – http://www.youtube.com/c/JackTheRipperTours

"I'm not a butcher, I'm not a Yid, not yet a foreign skipper, but I'm your own light-hearted friend, yours truly, Jack the Ripper,"

CHAPTER 12
PAUL BEGG (Jack the Ripper expert)

The first time I heard the name Jack the Ripper I was catching a late-night discussion programme with Donald MacCormick on the telly in the 1960s. Donald actually published a book in 1959 called 'The Identity of Jack the Ripper' so he knew his stuff. He released that same book again in the early 1970s. Watching that programme about the Whitechapel killings was my introduction to Jack, I have no idea why I was even allowed to be up so late to watch it, but that's where it started. I bought Donald's book from a bookshop in Cardiff. I got the book home and read it yet didn't understand a word of it but at the same time it fascinated me all the same. It was in the late 60s or early 70s when Jack the Ripper properly penetrated my brain and I could take it all in and understood fully.

Over the years, I would buy every Jack the Ripper book as they were published by the likes of Robin Odell, Tom Cullen, Stephen Knight and various Donald Rumbelow books. Many years on from reading the books, my wife was working for Westwood Television and Colin Wilson, who is an English writer who has written about Jack, was there, that made me desperate to go along and talk to Colin. Sadly, I never got the chance on that occasion but years later when I started doing my own things on Jack, we spoke many times before he died in 2013.

Today, because there are so many self-publishing writers there seems to be a book about Jack the Ripper every month.

Researching Jack the Ripper was very different back in the 1970s/80s than today because everybody has the internet now which makes it so much easier. Back then it was so difficult to gather information for us researchers. Today we've got things such as digitised newspapers from the old archives.

I would classify Jack the Ripper more of a mystery than true crime. The thing that draws the curious public to the whole case now is the mysterious element rather than the horrible acts. Once someone finds out about the murders, often they'll drift away to other murder cases. Those who stay and just become obsessed with the whole Whitechapel story then focus on other pointers of the case such as Victorian times, other suspects and the London Metropolitan police etc... With the killings of 1888 never being solved, people have managed to come along over the years and develop the story in a totally different direction.

Since the centenary year the myth of the Ripper has developed with various radio programs, books, films, documentaries etc... Inside that myth stands a tall man all dressed in black wearing a top hat, cape, waistcoat and carries a stick and a little bag to go with it. The reality of it is now in 2022, 134 years on that the whole Jack the Ripper image hasn't really moved on, and we're no closer to knowing the truth. He looked completely different to what the books and films tell us he looked like.

Many decades ago, now the Ten Bells pub in Spitalfields changed its name to Jack the Ripper. This led to several campaigns from women largely saying that it was outrageous. I don't think they fully understood that this wasn't celebrating the serial killer of 1888, it was more so focusing on the social history of that part of the world.

I myself have written around 8 or 9 books with most of them being about Jack the Ripper. The reason most of them have been about Jack is largely because the publishing companies wouldn't let me cover anything else, meaning murder sells! If ever I tried to suggest a different topic other than the Whitechapel killings, then the opportunities became few and far between. I have managed to slip the odd book on the history of the C.I.D, the mystery of the Marie Celeste and how people disappear but the rest have been on the ripper.

Over the years, I've spent so much time in Whitechapel, and there was a time when, if there was a Jack the Ripper documentary on the telly, nine times out of ten I'd pop up on it because I've done that many. Many of my friends said you couldn't watch anything on Jack without Paul Begg being involved. I do feel a special connection with the area of Whitechapel. You either feel it or you don't! I can't explain to all you readers what feeling Whitechapel means but there is something special. To many it may be a bit of a dump with a busy market, then to others it's a deep dark well of hundreds of years of unique history behind it.

When I used to walk the streets of Whitechapel many years ago, I never used to view it as it was then, I was doing it as it used to be all those years ago. The complete district is a total fascination that one can't deny. If you know a little bit about the place like I do and many others do, you just can't grasp just how eerie it all is. Many years ago, when the old Grave Maurice on Whitechapel Road was open, I would often go and sit in it. I would stand there at the bar ordering my pint of beer and I'd just take it all in. Now the Grave Maurice wasn't the greatest pub on earth, but it was steeped in so much history very much like 'The Pride of Spitalfields' just off Brick Lane. I would meet a few of my fellow Ripperologists in there and also the Ten Bells when it was how it used to be. The Ten Bells was owned by a guy named Ernie. When I was in London good old Ernie would put me up for a week at a time. I did get quite pally with one of the Great Train

Robbers and I used to see Mad Frankie Fraser around the East End when I was in the area, but I wasn't a particular true crime fan, although that may sound a little bizarre because I've done several books on the Ripper. It's the unknown that surrounds Jack and the whole East End history going way back to Roman times is what I've covered extensively and even fairly heavyweight archaeology but never brutal true crime as such.

Some people think, because I'm viewed as an expert on the subject, that I'll have some inside information on who the killer was. I have to be brutality honest with you all, I really have no idea who the hell he was! There aren't any modern suggestions because forensics have gotten so much better over the last hundred years or so. If I had to stick my neck out and go down some line it would have to be the commissioner Sir Robert Anderson's view of being a low-class Polish Jew named Kosminski. I've seen all the documentation and even had it kept in my wardrobe for a short time. After speaking with other experts in the field I don't see any reason why I'd look elsewhere other than Kosminski. If he was the leading suspect for the Head of the C.I.D at the time and also a senior investigating officer in 1888 then it's good enough for me 134 years on. I imagine them officers would have had access to everything they needed, and these were very educated men.

Although the police thought it was a guy named Kosminski, today we can't even be sure of who this Kosminski fella really was. There must have been more evidence against him than any other guy in the frame from back in that day.

Stewart Evans who's a credible Ripperologist is convinced that not all the canonical were done by the same hand. He thinks that Liz Stride isn't a ripper victim and going by the modus-operandi he's correct. Then you take into account that there were very few murders in the East End at that time, yet you have two within the hour only half a mile apart, which is hard to believe for some people. The odds seem very much against those two murders actually being two separate killers.

In regard to Whitechapel, I haven't been back a lot in the last ten years because I'm now in a wheelchair. I suffered a spinal injury in 2013 which had left me needing wheels to get around those East End streets.

Today I'm 70 and I live in a little village in Wales, but I would hope to get to Whitechapel again. The area is changing so much, even over the last few years that I haven't been there. I look at pictures on social media at the likes of the new Whitechapel Tube Station. It is a special place as I've already said, and it will forever hold lots of wonderful memories for me.

It's because of Jack the Ripper that I've had the chance to meet the likes of Adam Wood, Keith Skinner and Martin Fido etc... It's been quite exciting to walk into the Jack the Ripper story and meet many of the main characters who know the most about it. Jack has been very good to me shall I say if that makes sense. It's because of Jack the Ripper that I was invited to travel to places as far as America along with other part of Europe, to do talks about him.

Although Martin Fido, Richard Jones, Mick Priestley and Donald Rumbelow did various tour guides along the streets of London, I've never liked the Jack the Ripper aspect side of things. I'm more of the boring dull ripper historian compared to the others out there who work on the case. I'm more interested in the facts/mystery of the whole case. The difference between me and the guys I've just mentioned is those guys did it as a career and a business, anything I did with Jack was a hobby so that's why I never felt the need to get involved as much as the others. I didn't want to get involved in the Jack the Ripper industry. I was involved because of a passion in the case and the whole East Enders history.

I do enjoy going to events such as the Whitechapel conferences and I've met some fabulous people such as the late Jeremy Beadle. He was very much involved in the Ripperology world.

The books I wrote on Jack were, Jack the Ripper – The Facts, Jack the Ripper – The Definitive History and Jack the Ripper – The A - Z. In fact, there's another I almost forgot which is called Jack the Ripper – The Forgotten Victims. At first, I didn't set out to write the books I have on Jack, it's kind of just happened. Regarding my books on Jack, Jack the Ripper – The Facts is just what you'd expect, the clues in the name and it looks at the solid truths. Jack the Ripper – The Definitive History was an attempt to set the Jack the Ripper murders in the context i.e., what else was happening in the country at the time. The crimes break up chapters such as the press coverage, the police investigation and prostitution/women's rights etc... It was done, effectively as a trilogy and then I added on Jack the Ripper – The Forgotten Victims, that book covers the non-canonical victims of Jack. The published work I've done covers the crimes, history and people of that time.

When anybody classifies anything as the world's greatest like the Jack the Ripper murders it hits home just how big a thing it is. Over in America they celebrate the gunfight at the O.K Corral. They'll have walking tours around Chicago where the St Valentines Massacre took place. These are awful things where people were killed but the East End of London in Tower Hamlet people stay away from it. I know it's a gruesome subject and violence against women can't be condoned, but none the less with Jack the Ripper, you're dealing with a historical story. I don't think the East End of London should ignore that.

These days the councils in the East End are working very hard to rub out these bits of history. For example, on the Spitalfields website they have recently been seeking donations to start up walks to show the other aspects of the East End. Basically, it shouldn't have a walk celebrating an unknown serial killer of the area once upon a time. The reality of it all is that in my opinion, Spitalfields is Jack the Ripper!!! Throughout the East End villains such as Ronnie & Reggie Kray, Jack 'spot' Comer, Roy Shaw, Lenny McLean etc... Its Jack the Ripper that stands at No.1 in East End folklore! It's very silly to ignore these parts of history because like it or not, these things went on. For instance, I don't like the glorification of the Kray Twins. These people meet up and rejoice over two nasty pieces of work like they are some kind of Robin Hood figures. Unlike Jack the Ripper there's no real mystery behind these two callous wicked men who went on to spend the rest of their lives in jail from the age of 34.

I understand the real East Enders who I've met not wanting the Krays to represent their area. At the same time the East End association, going as far back as I've ever dug, has been with crime. Take the 1838 Charles Dickens novel Oliver Twist. You've got old Fagin who's this Jewish character and receiver of stolen goods. Then there's the vicious thug Bill Sykes who walks around the East End shadowed by his bull-terrier dog Bullseye. In Dickens' novel he portrays Fagin's light-fingered boys going through Whitechapel on the rob. If you look at when that was written it was 50 years before Jack the Ripper came along in 1888, the area is stereotyped for all types of criminal conduct. There are various novels from the 1950's set in snooker halls in the East End and how Scotland Yard Detectives meet informers, but where do they meet? Aldgate tube station. The East End is deeply associated with crime although it doesn't happen as such anymore, but it used to be. It used to be the haunt of all kinds of activities from gangs such as the Bessarabian Tigers who were made up of Russian Jews. I remember going into the old Frying Pan pub with Martin Fido when it was still trading as a public house on Brick Lane. When I was in there with Martin it was its very last night as a pub in 1991 before it became a curry house. As me and Martin were sat there, we could hear conversations flowing of none other than pure uncut criminal activities such as narcotic sales, prostitution and gangland hits. One of the characters in there was a guy who went by the name of, 'Darkie the Coon' you rightly couldn't get away with using that terminology in 2022! "Darkie" would walk up and down Brick Lane with two guns in his holsters exactly like a cowboy. "Darkie" was one hell of a character as well as a gangster. Rumour has it on the East End grapevine "Darkie" had also been a war hero. At the time I didn't know who he even was, let alone just how dangerous he'd been or what he was even talking about because he was quite old at that point. Looking back on it know I wished I'd been aware of who that guy was. First of all, I'd have taken stack loads of photos of the pub of course because it was the last pub that Polly Nichols had been drinking in just before she was Jacks first victim, and two I'd have got photos of Darkie because in that environment, he was a real somebody. (AUTORS NOTE – after researching Darkie there was lots of old snippets of information of him. It's said he was allegedly a loan shark/pimp in the East End who dressed like a cowboy and walked around like he owned the place. Darkie had scars on his face from several gang fights over the years on Brick Lane.)

Today they make drama series on things such as the Peaky Blinders which were based in Birmingham, yet the East End wants to turn its back on its social history on people like Darkie (real name Isaac Bogard). The likes of Peaky Blinders are massively popular yet the councils in the East End would rather talk about museums. If you bring people into the area because of what the East End attracts, then the local economies would flourish. They should learn to love their own deficiencies.

Many of the pubs that I look back on with fondness were bloody awful really with murky pasts such as the Ten Bells, The Blind Beggar, Grave Maurice and The White Hart but it added to their character. Those pubs had a great feel to them. In those pubs in the East End there was a community and life about them. That very same community spirit which the Ten Bells had 30 odd years ago has vanished. All that is left is a shell of what it was. I remember the Ten Bells would have strippers in on an afternoon and on an evening so you can imagine how many tradesmen working locally would come in. It was very disconcerting being in the middle of a pub and a stark-naked girl questioning you about who Jack the Ripper really was!

My final say for this chapter is I'd like to say that the subject of Jack the Ripper is hugely important and if you're lucky like I am you'll feel that special feeling about Spitalfields and Whitechapel. That unique feeling separates it from the other parts of the great city of London that just don't compare to Whitechapel. If you walk the full length of Brick Lane and you get to the bottom end where the Jewish-style 24/7 Beigel Bake shop is, the feeling and mood changes. As soon as you walk past The Blind Beggar away from Whitechapel that magic feeling goes.

"NO DOUBT JACK THE RIPPER EXCUSED HIMSELF ON THE GROUNDS THAT IT WAS HUMAN NATURE."

A.A. Milne

CHAPTER 13
LINDSAY SIVITER HISTORIAN/RESEARCHER

I am originally from Birmingham in the West Midlands which is a long way from Whitechapel and it's quite a bizarre story how I got involved in the Jack the Ripper industry.

I was born in the famous summer heatwave of 1976 at the same time Stephen Knight's iconic book *'The Final Solution'* was being published. After school and college I went to Oxford Brookes University to study a History of Art Degree; I've always had a passion for History. Once qualified, I went to live in Paris and worked as a historian and archivist at a Cathedral for a year before moving back to Oxford. I then worked in a variety of museums and historic venues before finally moving to London to work for Discovery Tours as a Ripper guide and also at The Science Museum as a Visitor Services Assistant and freelance Egyptologist.

It has been many years now since I came to the bright lights of London after meeting my current boss, notable author and historian Richard Jones (featured in this book) at a party. Spookily, I had been watching Richard on a documentary that very same morning, and as I didn't think I would ever meet him it's fair to say I was a little starstruck. I had been a big fan of Richard's work for years and here he was, at this party standing in front of me, and the thing was, I had no idea that he was going to be there. After talking to Richard about Jack the Ripper for a while he just came out with, "well would you like to be one of my tour guides"? Richard literally offered me a job on the spot and bearing in mind that he didn't even know me, it was very generous of him. Twenty one years later I still proudly tread the cobbles in the East End guiding groups for Discovery Tours and am currently his longest serving Ripper guide.

Thinking back to how I first heard about Jack the Ripper, I remember it was a strange experience which ultimately changed my life. In October 1988, when I was just twelve years old, I watched the now iconic miniseries *'Jack the Ripper'* starring Michael Caine and Lewis Collins. After watching the concluding episode in my bedroom, I heard a voice say: "THIS MAN DID NOT DO THIS AND <u>YOU</u> HAVE TO PROVE IT", so I was set on a quest! This lifelong quest has led me to spend as much time as possible reading and studying the case and to research the first ever full-length biography of the suspect unmasked as the killer in the miniseries - Sir William Gull. It has been my life's work and mission to clear his name of these hurtful accusations of him being one of the most famous serial killers in history. My biography will prove he had nothing to do with these terrible crimes and I hope the book will help to restore his much-maligned reputation. I feel very lucky as I have been the first researcher allowed access to the Gull family archives in the possession of his descendants, the current Baronet living with his family in South Africa. A few years ago, they kindly invited me to stay with them to see Gull's personal letters, heirlooms and objects which was such a great privilege.

Going back to the voice I heard in my bedroom after I watched the Jack the Ripper film. For several years I have been an active member of the prestigious Ghost Club (founded in 1862) and The Society for Psychical Research (founded 1882), so I do believe in the paranormal and such like that but where that voice came from I have absolutely no idea. I don't think it was Sir William Gull himself, but it was somebody who told me I must be his voice and defender. Listening to that voice as a 12-year-old girl went on to shape my whole future because I subsequently went to my local library and read all the Jack the Ripper books I could get my hands on. By coincidence my teacher at school was talking about Jack the Ripper in my English class and by then I had researched so much over the past week I asked whether I could talk about the miniseries. With his permission I got up and taught my class about the film and the truth and myths of the real story and facts behind it. I had become a lecturer at twelve years old! (laughs).

From the day I started researching the case of the Whitechapel murders it became my main hobby. I just read and read and read everything I could trying to absorb as much as I could. In 1998 I joined the Cloak and Dagger club (now the Whitechapel Society) and all the way through my time in Oxford I studied the Ripper case just as much as the subject I had gone to university for. I am still an active member of the Society and have given various lectures and written numerous articles for their great magazine.

One of my highlights at such a young age was meeting and going on one of Donald Rumbelow's Ripper tours. As the years went by, I started meeting the real experts of the field and got to know more and more notable writers, researchers and other people in the industry. Subsequently I was asked to lecture and give presentations at various conferences and venues around the UK, and I have been overwhelmingly lucky to have been asked to talk at many prestigious venues. One of these was at New Scotland Yard for the Metropolitan Police History Society where I was invited to become one of their youngest speakers and later, I became their youngest member. Many years on I now proudly serve as a member of the committee for the society helping to organise speakers and events.

For five years I proudly worked at Scotland Yard's famous 'Black Museum' aka The Crime Museum, being kindly rewarded with various commendations for the many hours of unpaid work I undertook. During my time in the museum, I worked with a lot of incredibly interesting iconic objects from famous historical crimes. I got the opportunity to handle many infamous items such as the gun which jammed when Reggie Kray attempted to shoot Jack 'The Hat' McVitie at Evering Road. That gun was fished out of the canal in Bow but for many years was wrongly labelled on display as the weapon used to shoot George Cornell in the Blind Beggar Pub. However, having examined it I felt this was not the gun used in the Blind Beggar as it was too degraded. So, I spent several hours looking through twenty large boxes containing the original Kray trial files and discovered the evidence to prove my theory. That's what I love about being a historian. I'm a historical detective so I was able to piece together from the Kray files that the gun on display in the museum had the incorrect information. Also, in the museum in the Kray section, are their original mugshots and criminal record, a crossbow (which was never used) and a concealed weapon in a briefcase which had a needle at the bottom of it (also never used). The plan was for one of the Krays henchmen to walk up to the target from behind and jab him with the briefcase with a concealed needle containing poison. To anyone else around it would just look like the target had fainted or had a heart attack. The museum collection also has the torture box that the Krays rival gang, the Richardson's used on their victims. It's so funny because I attended a lunch with Eddie Richardson a few years ago and I told him that the museum had his torture device and he looked at me in amazement and said, "Can I have it back?" I simply replied: "Sadly not."

As part of my work in this famous private police training museum I helped re-organise displays, helped curate various exhibitions, handled many items from various criminal cases and assisted in the final packing up of all the museum objects when they had to be moved into temporary storage while waiting for their new current home to be created.

Over the years I also got to know several of the old detectives and other authorities such as Criminologist, TV personality and famous Curator of The Black Museum, Bill Waddell. I became good friends with Bill and his wife after his retirement in the last few years of his life and now they have both sadly passed. I was often invited round to their home in Sussex where Bill would spend hours regaling to me the most amazing stories from his time at the museum and as a serving policeman. He was another one of my heroes growing up and I had all his books and videos, but never did I think I would sit in his old office for five years! Another dream come true. I once asked Bill about the original Ripper police files and documents from 1888. He told me that although Scotland Yard moved in 1967 to modern skyscraper buildings in Victoria, (which have recently been demolished), all the Ripper files at the time when he joined as a young officer were still at the Victorian Scotland Yard building on Embankment just lying around in cardboard boxes along the corridor on the floor. I was astounded to hear this. The Yard didn't have an archive system so to speak for the really old historic files, everything was deteriorating on the floor. Bill said officers just used to walk past the boxes, occasionally enquiring about their contents and when being told they were files relating to the Jack the Ripper investigation, many just dipped in and took things as souvenirs. In 1988 the museum received two packages containing some of the original Ripper files and photographs and although one sender was identified as a relative of an officer who had recently passed away, the identity of the sender of the other parcel still remains a mystery to this day. Today, the surviving original police documents from the Ripper case are carefully preserved in the National Archives. However, the actual Suspect file (along with many other of the original files) have long gone on the Ripper case and are sadly still missing.

I personally like to have lots of different projects on the go regarding my Ripper research. One fascinating project is on Mr George Lusk, Chairman of the Whitechapel Vigilance Committee who, along with many other local businessmen in 1888 organised patrols for weeks for free in an attempt to catch the murderer. I am friends with George Lusk's great-great granddaughter, so I am researching a little booklet about him and his family.

Over the years I have contributed a variety of articles to various magazines and journals, providing knowledge of several East End characters connected with the Jack the Ripper murders, including possible victim Martha Tabram whose final resting place I discovered.

My forthcoming biography on Sir William Gull though will be my very first book that I've done fully completely on my own. You can see the name Lindsay Siviter as a contributor and researcher in many books, but I have never really had the confidence to do any on my own before but I'm starting to do that now. People often assume because my name is often mentioned in connection with the Ripper story, that I have written lots of books on the Whitechapel murders but that's sadly not the case. Lots of articles and lectures, but not yet a book, but hopefully that will change over the next few years! People also often see me as a familiar figure in the Ripper industry because firstly, when they attend Ripper related conferences I'm often there, and secondly because I have been involved with or featured in nearly 30 documentaries globally. I have been very lucky within the industry to have had so many opportunities.

Ever since my first visit to Whitechapel many years ago I have always felt a special sensation when I'm around this area because it's simply a magical place, especially in the heart of Spitalfields near Hawksmoor's famous Christ Church. That church has this magic pull on me for some reason. So does the famous pub opposite, the Ten Bells. The Ten Bells is such an iconic building and has a fascinating history which I plan to publish one day. My friend used to live upstairs in the pub and we both had experiences in there. From seeing the locks of the toilets moving on their own trapping us, physical manifestations of figures, footsteps with nobody there to being physically attacked by a spirit. One day I was at the top of a flight of stairs in the upper part of the building when I felt an invisible hand thump me on my back and push me. I swiftly fell down the stairs nearly breaking my arm. My friend who was living there eventually left due to all the negative paranormal occurrences he experienced. The Ten Bells is absolutely rife with spirits, and I'm not just talking about alcoholic ones. If anyone looks on YouTube and puts, 'Lindsay Siviter in the Ten Bells' they can watch my presentation explaining the details of what went on. What makes the place even more spooky is that there are no carpets whatsoever in the Ten Bells upstairs, so every creek and creep can be heard. Over the years several landlords have died in the pub including the one resident there at the time of the Ripper murders, John Waldron who strangely died the following year after the murders. Goodness knows how many hours over the last twenty years I have spent standing outside the pub with my groups talking and looking up at it and sharing my research on its history.

I often get asked the million dollar question: 'Who was Jack the Ripper?' but my honest opinion is I don't even think it's anyone we've heard of! After over 30 years of research I am still none the wiser, there just really isn't any conclusive evidence against anyone. However, one thing I do believe is that he was most likely a local person who knew the East End well so he could vanish into the shadows. The women clearly trusted him, he would have looked normal, unthreatening, like most serial killers do. For many people who come on the walking tours the most famous and well known theory that they like to discuss is the one known as 'The Royal Conspiracy Theory'.

This theory, most famously endorsed in Stephen Knight's highly influential book *The Final Solution* is I readily admit, a fantastic story. To this day it is still one of the bestselling books on Jack and one of my personal favourites, even though I know the story in many areas is very inaccurate. However, we have to remember the source for Knight's story was actually Joseph Sickert (allegedly the artist Walter Sickert's son). I myself became good friends with Joseph before he died in 2003 and spent many hours talking to him about his life and the Ripper story. I know others have said 'Joseph Sickert was a fraud' etc... but whatever you believe about Joseph, unless you had actually met the man it's not fair to judge him. Ultimately Joseph was so knowledgeable and passionate about this subject. Yes, he said a few things that after research were proved incorrect, but he was simply recounting a story which had been told to him as a young boy. He passionately believed what he had been told and was just repeating what he had heard. For example, before Joseph came along nobody had ever heard of a coachman called John Netley but he did exist. Many people might think Joseph made the whole story up for financial gain, but I can tell you right now that Joseph never made a penny from his family story. Stephen Knight betrayed him as he failed to honour their mutual monetary agreement. Joseph sadly never received anything because of his own naivety in not signing a legal contract. Joseph was very upset as he had promised to give his share of profits to the Deaf Centre because many members of his family are deaf, just like Princess Alexandra and Prince Albert Victor, who he claimed he was descended from were. THIS betrayal was the reason why Joseph later denied the story in the press. However, he realised many years later his denial was one of the worst mistakes he ever made because it destroyed his credibility. Joseph once told me he only did that on the advice of a certain journalist, and he deeply regretted it. I personally believe that there was something truthful within Joseph's story with a connection to the Royal Family. The grey area is just how it all connects to the Ripper story.

The really interesting thing for me is that Sir William Gull's name was not connected to this story in print until an article by Dr Thomas Stowell in The Criminologist magazine in November 1970 when it was suggested Gull had looked after the Ripper who was one of his patients. Some also believe that there were other hints mentioned in the article which seemed to point the finger of suspicion directly at Sir William himself. However, Sir William, as I will say in my book, had an alibi. I discovered that Sir William was so gravely ill in the April of 1888, he could not get out of his bed, to get into a carriage, to go round the corner to see his only daughter get married. I also discovered he was not even in London at the time of the murders as from the late summer until the late autumn in 1888 he was recuperating at a house in the Surrey countryside. Gull was not Jack the Ripper.... time to let him rest in peace.

Over the years there have been so many coincidences that I often get the feeling Sir William is looking down on me, even helping me. To give you just one example of this, one day when I was working in a museum archive in Oxfordshire, I found a note on my desk which read, 'I'm really sorry Lindsay but I've had to put this object on your desk, please feel free to use one of the other desks'. I went to look and there was this great big, massive old long metal box. Looking closer, I saw it was a metal case badly scratched and worn. When I opened it what I discovered inside was a beautiful black velvet Victorian Court suit with a waistcoat, breeches, jacket and other features, all with stunning shiny buttons along with a highly decorated cocked hat. I thought 'this is wonderful I wonder who it belonged to and where it's come from!' I was told it had recently been donated by a local drama society who had been wearing it as a pirate's outfit! They had offered it to the Oxfordshire archives because of the link to the cut steel buttons which they believed were made locally in Woodstock. However, this later turned out to not be the case as they were made in my hometown.

When I asked my colleagues who these items belonged to, they told me they hadn't been able to trace the identity of the name on the lid. As I closed the lid, I saw the name *Sir W. Gutt Bt.* I suddenly realised that it didn't say Gutt, it said Gull! There was a huge scratch through the Ls that made them look like Ts. It was only then that the penny dropped, and I said, 'O MY GOD! DO YOU KNOW WHO THIS SUIT BELONGS TO?, IT BELONGS TO SIR WILLIAM GULL'! The name meant nothing to my colleagues until I told them I was writing his biography and they were quite shocked as was I! Subsequently I researched the tailors who made the suit which had accidently landed on my desk and found that they still existed. Not only that but I discovered in their records that this suit had landed on my desk the day it was made over a hundred years earlier AND was possibly the most important suit of Gull's life as it was the one he had specially made and indeed wore when he received his baronetcy in 1872! As his biographer to have all of this new information was amazing. This is what I mean when I say I feel Gull has helped me along the way, some sort of divine intervention perhaps.

If I had never watched the Michael Caine film as a child back in 1988, my life would have been completely different. When I started doing the Ripper walking tours around the East End I was the same age as victim Mary Jane Kelly (25). Next year I will be the same age as victim Annie Chapman (47) and that feels so surreal. I'm one of a few historians who each year on the anniversary of their deaths, visit the victims' graves to lay flowers, tidy their final resting places and pay our respects. I personally also do the latter on all my tours.

People then and now have always been fascinated with the Whitechapel murders and I do not think this interest will end anytime soon. Sadly, what is ending and changing forever is the landscape of the East End itself. Today in 2022 all the murder sites have practically gone or changed beyond recognition so you

135

can only imagine just how different the place is going to be in another 50 years! On my walking tours I show visitors historical images of the places and sites we go to as they once looked. I think it's really important as a guide to help reconstruct these scenes for people as best I can and to try help visitors visualise the area in the Ripper's time in order for them to understand and appreciate the story more. For historians geographical and topographical research is vital. Visiting places and following in the footsteps of people from the past, enables I believe, history to be brought back to life in an attempt to understand it more fully and, who knows, where possible to learn from its mistakes.

Concluding on Whitechapel as an area, I would say there's something incredibly hypnotic about the place. Though I have travelled the world, I feel most at home in Whitechapel and Spitalfields. The very first time I was shown around by a friend, I bizarrely already knew where everything was, it was though I had an internal map. Maybe I had a past life there, but I have always felt extremely comfortable and had an affinity with the place. I've been lucky in getting to know this particular part of London very well after spending over twenty years as a tour guide, but I'm still learning new things and I hope I always will.

"IN LONDON EVERYONE IS DIFFERENT, AND THAT MEANS ANYONE CAN FIT IN."

Paddington Bear

CHAPTER 14
THE TOP 3 SUSPECTS OF THE VICTORIAN POLICE ON WHO THEY THOUGHT WAS JACK

MONTAGUE JOHN DRUITT came from an upper-middle-class English background and studied at Winchester College and the University of Oxford. After graduating, he was employed as an assistant schoolmaster at a boarding school and pursued a parallel career in law, qualifying as a barrister in 1885. His main interest outside work was cricket, which he played with many leading players of the time, including Lord Harris and Francis Lacey.

In November 1888, Druitt lost his post at the school for reasons that remain unclear. One month later his body was discovered drowned in the river Thames. His death, which was found to be suicide, roughly coincided with the end of the murders attributed to Jack the Ripper. Private suggestions in the 1890s that he could have committed the crimes became free information to the public during the 1960s and then he would go on to be named in several books as a possible killer. The evidence against him was entirely circumstantial, however, even though his own family thought he was the killer, many Ripperologists reject him as a serious suspect.

AARON KOSMINSKI was a Polish Jew who came from Poland in the 1880s. He worked as a barber in Whitechapel in the East End. From 1891, Kosminski was institutionalised after he threatened his sister with a knife. He was held at Colney Hatch Lunatic asylum, then transferred to Leavesden Asylum.

Police from the time of the murders named one of their suspects as "Kosminski" and described him as a Polish Jew in an asylum. One hundred years later after the murders, the suspect

"Kosminski" was identified as Aaron Kosminski, but there was little evidence to connect him with the "Kosminski" who was suspected of the murders, and their dates of death were different. The probability was Kosminski was confused with another Polish Jew the same age named David Cohen who was extremely violent at the Colney Hatch Asylum.

In 2014, Ripperologist Russell Edwards claimed in a book, 'Naming Jack the Ripper', that he proved Kosminski's guilt. In 2007, he bought a shawl which he believed to have been left at a murder scene and gave it to biochemist Jari Louhelainen to test for DNA. A peer-reviewed article on the DNA was published in 2019. However, scientists from Australia have criticised the paper and its conclusions, pointing to a number of errors and assumptions by the author.

MICHAEL OSTROG was a Russian criminal first proposed by Sir Melville Macnaghten in 1894.

Ostrog was a known swindler with a heavy criminal record, mainly for scams and frauds, but never anything of a serious nature after that. According to recent investigations, back in 1888 he was imprisoned in France, which rules him out of his participation in any of the Jack the Ripper killings.

MY NO.1 SUSPECT IN THE CASE
CHARLES ALLEN LECHMERE (CROSS)

Charles Lechmere was long regarded as merely an innocent witness who found the body of Mark Ann Nichols, the first of the five Ripper victims, accidently on his route to work. The suggestion that that he could actually have been Jack was first raised by Derek Osbourne around the millennium in a True Crime magazine. The following year saw the possibility further explored by John Carey, while Osbourne went on to examine a set of remarkable coincidences as all five murders were done not only on his route to work, but also on his only day off a week.

In the last few years mainstream awareness has grown on this possible killer. Lechmere is not only linked to the Whitechapel murders, but also the Thames Torso murders. After studying this case for more than 30 years now, my 'favourite' suspect without a shadow of a doubt is Charles Lechmere... Then again, I could name another two-dozen like I have this and present a case and you'd think it could be any of them also.

It's the reason why this whole case is so gripping, captivating and grossly intriguing... It's NEVER EVER going to be solved! I doubt that Whitechapel will ever escape its sordid past, but it should NEVER put a black mark against its bright future! Jack's five killings shouldn't tar the area as there are good things it has produced, such as the birth of the Salvation Army which came from 272 Whitechapel Road. No area in the country is perfect, Whitechapel deserves to be allowed to flourish like every other area of London and not be a victim of its dark history any longer.

According to new research the East End accent will disappear from the London streets within 30 years from now and the

Cockney accent will be 'brown bread'. Cockney will be replaced by multicultural London English – a mixture of Cockney, Bangladeshi and West Indian accents. The Cockney sparrow (refers to the archetype of a cheerful, talkative Cockney) will be no more, but as Chris Ross, The East End Poet says in his chapter, change is inevitable in life, we've just got to roll with the punches!

Today, in Scotland Yard's official files lies 167 possible suspects names. Back in 1888 over 2,000 people were interviewed, over 300 were investigated and 80 were detained. If they couldn't find him 134 years ago then I'm sure we won't find the most written about killer in history now, but it won't put us all off from completely being smitten with the case, I'm sure!

"I NEVER FEEL SO ALIVE AS WHEN I WALK THE STREETS OF WHITECHAPEL ONCE A YEAR... I DON'T THINK I'LL EVER BE ABLE TO GIVE MY HOLIDAY'S ON THE MANOR UP AS LONG AS I'M ON THIS PLANET... ISN'T WHITECHAPEL TRULY BLOODY BRILLIANT."

Jamie Boyle Author
P.S. THANK YOU FOR READING THIS BOOK. PPS MAYBE ITS BECAUSE I'M AN ADOPTED LONDONER

THE VICTORIAN VILLAN
by Lord Josh Allen

There is a murderer roaming the streets tonight, bathed in mist that lurks in the shadows not the light

Wearing formal attire, he appears to be respectable, this clever disguise renders him undetectable

Praying upon the woman of Whitechapel with a soul rotten to the core like that of an apple

His ghostly silhouette is often seen by passers-by, could it be the slasher or simply the trick of an eye,

His unsuspecting victims thought he was a punter, how could they know he was a brutal hunter,

For their services he would always leave a shilling, right before he opened his briefcase to finish a killing,

The police were puzzled and begin to question who, this gentleman killer was far too clever to leave a clue,

One by one the bloodied bodies continued to pile, each more gruesome, disgusting and horribly vile,

A lengthy investigation was already underway, the people of London were working night and day,

To catch an assassin who was most skilled, a sickening predator obviously thrilled,

Years went by and the case remained unsolved, slowly but surely all the leads went cold,

Had this madman truly escaped the grasp of the law, people began to rest easy but how can they be sure,

Perhaps he's still walking the alleys of the East End, if you mention his name, you're sure to offend,

Nobodies likely to forget his heinous crimes, not even in these advanced modern times,

Will we ever find out the identity of the man in black, the infamous monster ripper only known as Jack.

"NOTHING IS CERTAIN IN LONDON BUT EXSPENSE."

William Shenstone

WHITECHAPEL
by Chris Ross
The East End Poet

If you drive along Commercial Road and get to Gardiners corner it doesn't look like it used to look and I thought I'd better warn ya!

The roundabouts not there no more, though Leman Street's still one way and you can't turn down Middlesex Street, I tried the other day.

Tubby Isaac's stall has gone, and Blooms has closed as well and now the foundry's closing where they made the Liberty Bell but the Indian food's still pukka if you walk along Brick Lane, I had a ruby there last night and I'll go back there again.

In Wentworth Street and Fashion Street nothing much has changed, it's just the way the traffic moves that been, well... rearranged.

London Hospital has been moved a bit, its behind where it used to be, but the remnants of our yesterdays are there for all to see.

While everything is different most things look the same, some pubs survive and stay alive with just a change of name.

The cycle superhighway makes the traffic even worse, as ever though you'll always find a doctor or a nurse.

The station and market stalls, the shops along the waste, The Beggars on the corner though, the brewery's been displaced.

If you drive along Commercial Road and get to Gardiners corner, it doesn't look like it used to look, and I thought I'd better warn ya'

WHITECHAPEL – HOME OF SUSPECTS, LUNATICS & A LEATHER APRON...

ALSO A FEW FAMOUS PEOPLE FROM THERE INCLUDE -

Damon Albarn – lead singer of British pop band Blur

Ashley Cole – Chelsea and England footballer

Jack Kid Berg – Boxer, "The Whitechapel Windmill" British Lightweight Champion 1934

Jack "Spot" Comer Jewish East End gangster and anti-fascist 1912 – 1996

Joseph Barnett – Jack the Ripper suspect and ex-partner of 5th victim Mary Jane Kelly

Aaron Kosminski – Polish Jew Barber and No.1 suspect in the Jack the Ripper murders

Micky Flanagan – comedian

Muzzy Izzet – former Leicester City footballer

Julius Stafford Baker – Cartoonist

Abraham Beame – first Jewish mayor of New York City

1906 – 2001

Stanley Black – Bandleader

1913 – 2002

Simon Blumenfeld – Novelist, Playwright and Columnist,

1907 – 2005

Georgia Brown (born Lillian Klot), Actress and Singer,

1933 – 1992

Tina Charles – 1970s Disco Artist, born 1954

Peter Cheyney – Mystery Writer and Journalist,

1896 – 1951

Jack Cohen, Angelo-Jewish businessman who founded the Tesco supermarket chain,

1898 – 1979

Roger Delgado – Actor (known for playing "The Master" in Doctor Who) 1918 – 1973

Lloyd Doyley – Footballer

Bud Flanagan, (born Chaim Reuven Weintrop), Music Hall comedian on stage, radio. Film and television,

1896 – 1968

Kenney Jones – Drummer in The Small Faces and The Who

Morris Kestelman – artist

Emanuel Litvinoff – Angelo-Jewish author

Gary Webster – EastEnders actor

RESIDENTS IN OR OTHERWISE ASSOCIATED WITH WHITECHAPEL

Catherine and William Booth – founders of The Salvation Army and statues of both are in Whitechapel today

Joseph Merrick – The Elephant man 1862 – 1890. Although born in Leicester, he saw out his final days in Whitechapel

Captain James Cook – Although from Middlesbrough, Britain's most celebrated explorer lived at 88 Mile End Road from 1764 until his death in 1779. Cook lived in Whitechapel when the place was still a nice semi-rural area. It wasn't until a century later that it turned into a Victorian overcrowded slum hellhole it's so often described in the history books

Altab Ali – murdered in Whitechapel Park in 1978 in a racist killing by 3 teenagers. The brutal murder brought the Bangladeshi community together and a church garden was subsequently renamed the Altab Ali Park in his memory.

Jack the Ripper – Serial killer. Say no more!

Jack London – Author who wrote 'The People of The Abyss' while staying in Whitechapel – an account of his 1902 stay amongst the East End poor

Vladimir Lenin – Instigator of the Russian Revolution. Vladimir lived in Whitechapel in the early part of the 19th century and would often be seen in several of the local pubs on Whitechapel Road

The grim 1888 Whitechapel murders have given the area eternal 'fame'. But also, the daily struggle of the souls roaming its crowded streets served as inspiration for numerous authors such as Charles Dickens.

A LIST OF OTHER PROPER NOTABLE COCKNEY'S

Steven Berkoff – British actor, author, playwright, theatre practitioner and theatre director. (Stepney)

Ledley King – former Footballer for Tottenham Hotspur. (Bow)

Dizzee Rascal – Grime MC. (Bow)

Eddie Marsan – English award-winning actor. (Bethnal Green)

Dame Barbara Winsor DBE – English actress. (Shoreditch)

Harry Redknapp – former Footballer and manager. (Poplar)

Mike Reid – Actor and comedian. (Hackney)

Roy 'Pretty Boy' Shaw – Author, businessman and former criminal. (Stepney)

Des O'Connor – Television personality and singer. (Stepney)

Lenny McLean – Bareknuckle/unlicenced boxer. (Hoxton)

Craig Fairbrass - English actor. (Mile End)

Samantha Fox – pop singer and glamour model. (Mile End)

Jamie Foreman – English actor. (Bermondsey)

Dave Courtney – Author and former gangster. (Bermondsey)

Rylan Clark – Television personality. (Stepney)

Eric Bristow AKA the crafty Cockney – Darts player. (Hackney)

John L Gardner – British, Commonwealth & European Heavyweight Champion Boxer. (Hackney)

John H Stracey – Boxing world champion. (Bethnal Green)

Charlie Magri – Boxing world champion. (Mile End)

Lord Alan Sugar – British businessman. (Hackney)

Martine McCutcheon -British actress and singer. (Hackney)

Dominic Negus - former Boxer and debt collector. (Bethnal Green)

Jade Goody - Big Brother contestant. (Bermondsey)

David Haye - former World Champion Boxer. (Bermondsey)

Michael Barrymore - television personality. (Bermondsey)

Tinchy Stryder -British rapper. (Bow)

Tony Mortimer - East 17 singer. (Mile End)

Jeremy Beadle television personality. (Hackney)

Freddie Foreman - former gangster. (Bermondsey)

Billy Murray - British actor. (Bethnal Green)

Patsy Palmer - British actress. (Bethnal Green)

Audley Harrison - British heavyweight boxer. (Bethnal Green)

"OH, I LOVE LONDON SOCIETY! IT IS ENTIRELY COMPOSED NOW OF BEAUTIFUL IDIOTS AND BRILLIANT LUNATICS. JUST WHAT SOCIETY SHOULD BE."

Benjamin Disraeli

WHITECHAPEL

Population – 14,862 as of 2011

London borough – Tower Hamlets

Ceremonial county – Greater London

Region – London

Postcode district – E1

Dialling code – 020

Police – Metropolitan

UK Parliament – Bethnal Green & Bow

London Assembly – City & East

PRODUCT OF A POSTCODE
AVAILABLE FROM AMAZON

Gary Hutton's autobiography is the story of an East End bloke's life and experiences. He shares his story of having a very tough upbringing in a large family and learning through his surroundings because that is all he saw and knew. Gary is a survivor and some of his experiences were not on the right side of the law, but to him it was the 'norm'. This is a story of a young boy who was taught to steal by the person who should have been his role model and mentor. Being taught the wrong way led to Gary turning into a young man who went down the path of crime which in turn led to incarceration. While imprisoned Gary did what he does best and survived but struggled with what was happening on the outside world and in particular his family. He is now a man who does his best to help others in any way he can through mentoring and talking to troubled young people heading down the same path he found himself on in his younger years.

This story contains a whole bag of emotions which will touch every reader; sadness, anger, disgust, trust, surprise and amusement to name a few. Not many could say they have lived such a life, maybe little snippets, but for all this to be packed in to 46 years may be too much for some to take.

Jack the Ripper's East End by Richard Jones & Adam Wood

Edgar's Guide to Jack the Ripper's East End is the ultimate tour around the sites of the infamous Whitechapel Murders. It enables you to visit all but one of the eleven murder sites and delve deeper into the backstreets of Spitalfields and Whitechapel than you would ever think possible. In so doing you will see much more of the real East End, and venture into places that have changed little, if at all, since the Ripper prowled their shadows. But this is not just a traditional guidebook; this is a full history of the Whitechapel murders. As you make your way around the route, you will be learning more of the story with every step taken, uncovering the fascinating story in the streets and at the very locations where it unfolded. Indeed, the history contained in this 200-page book is so detailed, that you can enjoy it without even venturing out to take the tour, making it the perfect addition to the library of the most ardent armchair detective. Another first offered by this Edgar's Guide is a separate tour - done by bus, train and Underground - that allows you to visit the graves of the five 'canonical' victims - Mary Ann Nichols, Annie Chapman, Elizabeth Stride, Catherine Eddowes and Mary Kelly. No other guidebook offers you this poignant opportunity.

AVAILABLE FROM AMAZON

OTHER BOOKS ON JACK THE RIPPER TO BUY –

"One Autumn in Whitechapel" is the eagerly-awaited Jack the Ripper epic by M.P. Priestley – entirely, and exclusively, from the original reports. Four years in the making, there are no conspiracy theories or wild guesses in the book – the entire text is exclusively from original accounts, cross-referenced with modern-day profiling, serial killer/murder unit methods and techniques to, for the first time, expose the grim, historically-accurate reality of the events that took place and the man who committed them.

It's in the detail that has never been seen before, and a new prime suspect is revealed – a suspect who hid in plain sight the entire time, lived in the local area, and fits every characteristic of a serial, sexually-motivated offender that would be looked for today. The case is presented in exquisite detail, and, unlike with other accounts that claim to name a suspect, the evidence against him is very strong. The author, M.P. Priestley, has appeared via numerous channels as an expert to speak of Jack the Ripper and serial killers – namely on CNN, CBS, and channels as far afield as Brazil, South Korea and Iran. "One Autumn in Whitechapel" is the definitive account of the "Jack the Ripper" case and finally, through an exhaustive exploration of thousands of sources, and the use of modern-day crime scene investigation and profiling techniques, once and for all, REALLY does name the man that committed the notorious crime.

"SIMPLY BRILLIANT" – Fred Dinenage

"You must add this book to your collection and read it from cover to cover" – Dr. Katherine Ramsland, PhD, Forensic Psychologist, author of 'The Human Predator'

"I've met so many experts, and I've never met anybody who is as much of an expert on his subject as this guy is." – Charlie Sheen

UK True Crime Conference 2017 Book of The Year

YOU CAN BUY ONE AUTUMN IN WHITECHAPEL FROM ripperworld.net and etsy.com